EVALUATING WRITING

AN EVALUATION PROGRAM

a
publication
of

NATIONAL WRITING INSTITUTE
624 W. University #248
Denton, TX 76201-1889

ISBN 1-888344-05-9

Manufactured in the United States of America

For information, write: National Writing Institute
                            624 W. University #248
                            Denton, TX 76201-1889

                            call: 1 (800) 688-5375
                            e-mail: info@writingstrands.com

This book is dedicated to the parents who love their children enough to teach them at home.

NATIONAL WRITING INSTITUTE PUBLICATIONS
and
SERVICES

STUDENTS

Writing Strands Level 1
Writing Strands Level 2
Writing Strands Level 3
Writing Strands Level 4
Writing Strands Level 5
Writing Strands Level 6
Writing Strands Level 7
Writing Exposition
Creating Fiction

Communication And Interpersonal Relationships

————

Dragonslaying Is For Dreamers
Axel Meets The Blue Men
Axel's Challenge

PARENTS /TEACHERS

Evaluating Writing
Reading Strands

Teaching The Novel:
Dragonslaying Is For Dreamers

————

SERVICE

Correcting & Evaluation Service

ACKNOWLEDGMENT

I would like to acknowledge my debt to the homeschooling parents and their children who have taught me so much about the importance of love in the education equation. As a public school teacher for much of my adult life, I had great affection for my students—some I cared a great deal for—but not until I worked with my son did I realize what it meant to love a student.

I have seen so much love for children and love of teaching them in the homeschool groups that I have been privileged to work with in the last eleven years, that I have come to feel sorry for the children in institutions. What they are missing.

I have been truly moved by mothers who have cried in my workshops because they felt they couldn't give their children what they needed in educational experience. How much different were my experiences in the three decades of working in the public schools where the teachers made jokes about the children who had trouble learning and ignored their parents' efforts to become involved in their training.

In conventions I always see mothers carrying, nursing, loving, laughing with and holding the hands of their children. What good feelings that has brought to me. When I was still teaching in school and on the weekends on the road selling *Writing Strands* books, I reveled in all that parental love, and it helped me deal with the children in my school who would come with bruises from being trained by their parents. When I talked to my students who had been kicked out of their homes or who had run away from abusive situations, I would think of the loving relationships I would encounter in the coming weekend at a homeschool convention. Working with the parents of children who are loved has been a great pleasure to me and I thank you, homeschoolers, for that gift.

CONTENTS page

INTRODUCTION

I am often asked by homeschooling parents, "How do I evaluate my children's writing?" This is not an easy question for me to answer because I find evaluation challenging, even after 30 years of evaluating children's writing and talking to them about it.

But, this chore is much more different in public schools than it is at home. I found that when I began to work with my son's writing with him, I was looking at this problem much differently than I had been while in public schools. Public schools have problems that, fortunately, we don't have at home. In the classroom there are what are called standards for all children, and we know that many won't work because all children aren't the same. Also, there are the time constraints, which we don't have at home. There are 25 to 30 kids at a time who need attention, and they all have different problems with the language. In schools there are administrators who are motivated by politics and not by the needs of the children. There are curriculum demands that have to be met, even if they are unreasonable for some of the children. And, finally, there is the factory atmosphere in which children are seen as so many bodies that have to be processed every hour, five days a week, for 36 weeks each year. When I look at what I have just written, I am amazed that any of my students learned anything.

The idea that classrooms full of students are told that grades will be given on the basis of a curve or a class average is an insult to the idea of teaching. This means that on the first day the children are told that some of them have to fail. What an awful start for any project.

I have always found the whole idea of grading to be offensive to me and to my students. As much as I was able to do so, I kept the idea of grades from getting between my students and my teaching. This caused much trouble for the administrations under which I worked, but it was very beneficial for the kids.

How different it was to teach my son, Corey, at home. The only pressure I felt was the responsibility of teaching him to love and to use wisely his language. It never occurred to me that he might fail. I never once thought that he was not learning. I never had the idea that he was doing only an average job. I never gave him time limits to learn anything with the threat that if he didn't finish on time his grade would suffer or that I would think less of his ability.

You can have the same type of experience with your child. I think that the best advice I could give another homeschooling parent about this very difficult job is to ask you to think of your child's training and your evaluations as you would think about those two things when teaching your older children how to drive a car. You would not say to your children, "I am going to grade you kids on your driving on a bell curve, so, one of you has to fail and never drive at all." And, you wouldn't think that all of your children would have to learn each driving skill at the same rate or fail. You would say to each child, "I love you and want you to be a good driver so you'll not be hurt and won't hurt anyone else. I don't know how long this will take, but we'll work together with it until we both agree that you're an excellent driver."

You wouldn't give your children a C- on driving and then let them take the car. Assume the same attitude about grading writing. Help until they are excellent writers, or at least as good as they can be. It won't happen this year or maybe next year, but there will be improvement each year, and you'll have years together. One thing that makes it hard to think of teaching this way is that in writing there is no absolutely right way to say anything, just as there is no totally wrong way. There are just degrees of smoothness and economy and precision.

There are some things that children do need that I am sure you can give them. They need to feel good about what they do. This is just like you and me. We need this, too, and we're adults. This is one of the very good reasons that so many parents are homeschooling. Their kids weren't feeling good about what they were learning (or not learning) in school.

Making your children feel good about learning to write is not hard to do. It has a lot to do with your attitude as each child watches you react to what has been written. I think of it this way: if my wife made a list every night of all the things I did wrong during the day and told me how much I needed to learn, I would run away from home.

What kills children's desire to write is, when they put their hearts on a page—and this is exactly what they do when they write—and mom looks at it and says, "This is nice, but look at that spelling. You didn't learn anything about spelling all year. And the punctuation! We've got to get back to the basics of commas. Let me find my red pen and point out all of these errors for you." These children will want to run away from writing, and so would I.

An important thing to keep in mind is that children want to learn and want to please their parents. As a teacher, what a great position you're in. Find something absolutely wonderful about what has been written and ask your child to read that aloud. Then ask your child to read it to you. Then ask your husband or wife to read it. And then ask your child to read it to you both because you both think it's so beautiful. *Now* your child will feel good about what's been written. At this point, rather than point out all the things that are wrong with the paper, you can show one or two ways to make it even better. Say that the writing is almost perfect, and to make it perfect, you have one rule that you'd like to explain. Read that one rule and explain how it works. Help your child apply that rule to the writing. This will demonstrate what that application has done to that almost perfect sentence. Now, read it again and call it perfect! Your children will break their hearts trying to write perfect sentences for you.

If you take this approach, you can accomplish a number of things: your children will look forward to writing; they will not be afraid of making mistakes—and be white knuckle writers—they will learn the rules as they apply to their writing; and, they will feel good about what they are learning. The most important benefit of all is, they will learn to love their language.

I tried to do this in the public school and met with lots of resistance from the office and the other teachers, but with my son it worked just this way, and it can work this way for you, too. How wonderful it is to help people we love and who love us.

SOME CONDITIONS THAT MAKE HARD
THE TEACHING OF WRITING

FEAR AND INSECURITY are the two conditions that are the most damaging to writing competence for homeschoolers. These anxieties are felt not only by the students but many homeschooling parents as well.

When a parent expresses doubt about the ability to write, that doubt is sure to transmit to the child. It's logical that the child might say, "If Mom is unsure how to write well, I don't stand a chance of learning." I am sure that this is one of the reasons for the popularity of the grammar programs. If a parent uses a grammar drilling program instead of a writing program, it's much easier to be competent, for the answers are in the manual, and the work is either right or wrong.

This same condition is found in public schools. Very few teachers teach writing. Most teach grammar, spelling, and reading. Compared to teaching writing, these subjects, especially with teacher's answer keys, are easy to teach, and so it's easy to feel like an expert or to at least have confidence that the job can be done.

I don't want you to think that you can't teach writing—you can. What you have to have is a program of instruction that the child can start with at an appropriate level which has steps that are easy to follow and lead to the production of essays, reports, descriptions, and pieces of fiction. With such a program, if it has models as examples and detailed directions, you can help your children become competent writers.

What you need to do is get rid of fear and insecurity. You've chosen to work with *Writing Strands*, and so you have the conditions available to help your children. Now you have to help them understand that with this program they can succeed. This book was designed to give you just that help.

Most of the following conditions that inhibit clear writing are either produced by or made more severe by fears and insecurities. Read carefully the scope and sequence of the *Writing Strands* series near the back of this book. It should give you confidence that if your children finish the series they will have mastered the skills they will need to be good writers. If you follow the advice in this book, you'll transmit your confidence to your children, and you'll be able to convince them that not only can you teach writing but that they can learn to write.

MOTIVATION is a problem for some children. They don't see the importance of writing. This condition is most often found in families where the parents don't read. I don't mean that they don't read at all. They might read the *TV Guide* or the newspaper, but that their children don't see them sitting and reading books. It doesn't matter much what the subjects are, as long as children see their parents reading, they will want to read and will see value in the written word.

This is seen as very difficult by many homeschooling parents, because they truly are very busy. But, all it takes is ten minutes every evening. We all can afford that much time when the stakes are so great. If your children see Mom and Dad sitting down with

1

books for ten minutes each night after dinner, and they see that they let nothing interfere with their "reading time," the children will soon accept the value of words on paper.

One of the best things I was ever able to do for Corey, my son, was to give the TV away when he was about one year old. We didn't have TV in the house until he was 14. He watched his mother and father read to themselves, to each other and to him from the first day home from the hospital. By the time he was old enough to hold a book, he wanted his own. He was eager to learn to read and just as eager to learn to write. This is one thing you can give your children that takes no training whatsoever. There probably is little of more value that you could give to your children than a love of reading and writing.

CONCENTRATION is a problem for many children. If the problems with concentration are not clinical, there are some things you can do to help. Concentration is greatly aided by focus. The child has to know what to do, how to do it, where to do it, when to do it, and that it is possible to do it. If these conditions are present, the concentration necessary for the completion of the exercises in *Writing Strands* lessons will not be hard to handle. Most of these conditions are present in the lessons. You must provide the "where to do it, when to do it," and convince your child that it is "possible to do it." If each child is given a time to write, a place to write that is distraction free, and your encouragement by showing that you feel great confidence in your children's ability, then it will be possible for your children to focus enough to concentrate for the short periods of time necessary to do the daily work in *Writing Strands* lessons.

THINKING THROUGH IDEAS so they can be presented is a problem for many young writers. This usually happens when children have been asked to write and haven't been told how to do it. If you recognize yourself here, don't feel badly, this is an extremely common problem, even among teachers in school. After teaching writing for 30 years, I can count on half the fingers of one hand those English teachers who taught their students how to write. Many of them gave their students writing assignments but not instruction in how to put the words together.

This problem doesn't have to be yours any longer. The lessons your children are working with solve this for you. They are being shown how to do each assignment. As long as you don't become an anxious parent/teacher and worry about their papers being perfect, you and they should have no trouble with this any longer.

The lessons in *Writing Strands* have been designed to help the students think through the process of the production of each paper. When I wrote the assignments I was aware that this material was not elsewhere available to the children and their parents but that it was needed. I understood that most homeschooling parents are not English teachers, and created the necessary thought processes to solve this problem for you and your children.

TALKING ABOUT MECHANICAL PROBLEMS with your children need not be the most stressful time of the day. I discuss this problem in other places in this book, and you should look there if this is a problem for your children. The important thing to keep in mind is that your children will be with you for years, and they don't have to write perfect papers today, or this week or this year. They'll get frustrated if you point out everything they do that's wrong. Pick one mechanical problem this week and let the rest slide. Next week pick another one and let the rest slide. Soon you'll have covered the major ones and without all the frustration.

FOLLOWING DIRECTIONS is a big problem with many young writers. That's why I started the *Level Three* book with an assignment designed to teach young people that they can follow directions and be successful. If you haven't had a chance to use that exercise, that's okay. Try this: have them read all of any assignment and then tell you what they think they'll be doing. Then ask them to tell you how they plan to start. If they don't talk about starting as the exercise suggests, read the beginning of the exercise with them. Ask them again how they plan on starting. Do this until they get the idea that the directions say what they mean and do tell them exactly what to do. Have them start and then check that they are on the right path. Lots of congratulations. Praise will do it. They need confidence that they can follow directions. No exasperation or impatience on your part will ever help them.

NOT WANTING TO REWRITE is understandable. Especially for young writers. It's a lot of work. I don't like doing it and I've been writing for years. It's hard but necessary. If you approach rough drafts as just that, *rough*, and allow them to remain rough (your children will recognize this), then cleaning them up won't be such a big job. It's when they give you a paper that they have tried to make complete that they're blown away by your comments about all the problems.

A rough draft *should* have lots of problems in it. It's not supposed to be pretty and the spelling is not supposed to be perfect. There should be cross-outs and missed periods. It's just your children getting ideas down on paper. It's your children's thoughts on paper about the subject. Give your children a chance to correct all the problems before you comment on them.

A word processor is a wonderful thing for children to use for writing. It makes rewriting so easy. They're not expensive anymore and will be used for years. It's hard to rewrite with a pencil.

"I DON'T WANT TO WRITE!" is not an uncommon thing to hear in many homes. I've found that sometimes this is the case when the child has written and someone has belittled the effort. "Is that all you can think of?. . .What have you been doing all this time?. . .Did you get this paper out of the garbage?. . .Did the dog help you write this?
. . .I can't read this!. . .Is this the best you can do?" or "There sure are a lot of things wrong with this; let's find them."

How much better for a child if this is a parent's response, "Done already? You sure must be good at this writing stuff. . .I'm so proud of what you've done. . .Read that sentence to me. I think it's beautiful." Even if you have to search very hard for something nice to say about your child's writing, it's important to do so. Say good things and then find **one** thing that, if changed, might make the writing even better. Remember—one thing each week. More on this later. Your child will want to please you and get that praise. If the praise comes from writing, your child will want to write.

PROOFREADING is hard to do well. It takes practice, but there are some things you can do to help. Have your children read their papers aloud to you. Your children will hear mistakes when they read aloud that they'll miss when reading to themselves. If they don't catch the mistakes, you read to them from their papers. If this doesn't work, have them read their papers into a tape recorder. They should then be able to hear on the playback what the problems are.

While reading aloud, care should be taken that they read *exactly what's on the paper*. We all have the tendency to read what we *should have written* and not *the exact words* that are there. You might have to read over their shoulders to make sure of this, but it's worth it. They'll pick up the habit of proofreading aloud and thus catch many of their own mistakes. I still do this because it works for me.

COMMON WRITING PROBLEMS
and
HOW TO CORRECT THEM

There are two very important things to keep in mind when working with children and their writing:

1. All of us need to feel good about what we do. Children *must* feel good about their attempts to write.
2. You cannot correct all problems with one paper or all problems this week or this month, or even this year.

More on 1.

Every time your children write, find something absolutely wonderful about it. Your children should be eager to show you the results of their labor. There should be no fear that you'll only find fault with their work. Locate the best phrases, expressions, sentences, paragraphs, or ideas and talk to them about how well they are expressed. Have them read these wonderful words to you. Have them read them to Dad. Have Dad read them to the authors. Discuss why they were written as they were. Really enjoy the beauty of the words with them. Your children will be more ready to write next time and share their work with you.

More on 2.

If you find everything that's wrong with every paper, your children, like we would, will soon become discouraged. If you were to find one or two words each week that your child has to use often that were not spelled correctly, that would be enough spelling work for that week. In two or three years there would be a large spelling vocabulary of common words that the children would have at their command. More on this process later.

The same is true for mechanical problems. This week work on apostrophe use for contractions and next week work on apostrophe use for possession and the next week work on apostrophe use for showing the plural of letters, numbers and of words referred to as words.

Remember how long it took us to be perfect? Give your kids time, also.

WHAT TO LOOK FOR

Other than the obvious mechanical and spelling problems, there are things you can do to help your children write more smoothly, understandably, and efficiently. The first two rules apply here also. Find portions of a paper that are smooth and well written and point this out. Then pick one problem and explain the problem and demonstrate how the offending passage could be improved. Take it slowly. You'll be able to help your children for years.

PROBLEMS
WITH SENTENCE STRUCTURE AND WORD CHOICE

UNCONSCIOUS RHYMING:

The man was feeling really *well* until he *fell*. The rhyming words will ring bells in the reader's mind and detract from what the writer wants the reader to think about. That sentence should be re-written to read: *The man was feeling really well until he stumbled on the driveway and slid under the greasy truck.*

UNCONSCIOUS REPEATING OF WORDS OR PHRASES:

To *select magazines* which are written on the reader's level of reading and interest, a person should *select magazines* that reflect his economic and intellectual level.

This should be re-written to read:

Magazines should be selected to fit the reader's reading level and interest.

DICK AND JANE WRITING:

Writing is called this because of the way Dick and Jane books are written. *See Dick. See Jane. See Dick and Jane run. They are running to town.*

Magazine publishers print magazines for finely defined segments of the magazine reading public. The segments of the magazine reading public are identified by intellectual and economic indicators. These indicators are education and social position.

This should be re-written to read:

Magazine publishers print magazines for finely defined segments of the magazine reading public identified by the intellectual and economic indicators of education and social position.

OMITTED WORDS

Children often leave words out of sentences, or they leave the endings off of words. You can help them with this problem if you have them read their work out loud and slowly. Insist that they read slowly enough that you can catch every syllable. You may have to ask them to read sentences out loud to you five or six times before they catch the words they have left out. I have had kids in high school get angry after I had asked them to read aloud for the fifth or sixth time what they had written before they recognized what they had left out. Gentle patience works.

LISTING OF COMMON PROBLEMS

AMBIGUITY

A statement may be taken in two ways.

1. She saw the man walking down the street.

   This can mean either:
   A. *She saw the man when **she** was walking down the street; or,*
   B. *She saw the man when **he** was walking down the street.*

2. The use of pronouns *it, she, they, them* that do not have clear antecedents (what they refer to) can create ambiguous sentences:

   Bill looked at the coach when <u>he</u> got the money.

   This can mean either:
   A. *When Bill got the money **he** looked at the coach; or,*
   B. *Bill looked at him when **the coach** got the money.*

APOSTROPHE

An apostrophe (') is a mark used to indicate possession or contraction.

Rules:

1. To form the possessive case (who owns it) of a singular noun (one person or thing), add an apostrophe and an *s*.

   Example: *the girl's coat   Bill's ball   the car's tire*

2. To form the possessive case of a plural noun (two or more people or things) ending in *s*, add only the apostrophe.

   Example: *the boys' car*   *the cars' headlights*

3. Do not use an apostrophe for: *his, hers, its, ours, yours, theirs, whose.*

   Example: *The car was theirs.*   *The school must teach its students.*

4. Indefinite pronouns: (could be anyone) *one, everyone, everybody,* require an apostrophe and an *s* to show possession.

   Example: *One's* car is important.   That must be *somebody's* bat.

5. An apostrophe shows where letters have been omitted in a contraction (making one word out of two).

   Example: *can't* for cannot   *don't* for do not
   we've for we have   *doesn't* for does not

   Note that the apostrophe goes in the word where the letter or letters have been left out.

6. Use an apostrophe and an *s* to make the plural of letters, numbers and of words referred to as words.

   Example: There are three *b's* and two *m's* in that sentence.
   It was good back in the *1970's*.
   Do not say so many "*and so's*" when you explain things.

AUDIENCE

Writers don't just write. They write to selected readers in specific forms for purposes. To be effective, writers must decide what form is most appropriate for their intended readers so that they can accomplish their purposes.

Keep in mind that, just as your children talk differently to different audiences, they must write differently also. They would not talk to you or your minister the same way they would talk to each other or their friends.

As you read your children's writing, think of who their intended audiences are and try and judge how what they're saying will influence those people.

Examples:

1. Informal—colloquial (used with friends in friendly letters and notes):

   Man, that was a such a dumb test, I just flunked it.

2. Semiformal (used in themes, tests, and term papers in school and in letters and articles to businesses and newspapers):
   The test was very hard and so I did not do well.

3. Formal: (seldom used by students but appropriate for the most formal of written communication on the highest levels of government, business or education)

   The six-week's examination was of sufficient scope to challenge the knowledge of the best of the students in the class. Not being adequately prepared for it, I did not demonstrate my true ability.

AWKWARD WRITING

Awkward writing is rough and clumsy. It can be confusing to the reader and make the meaning unclear. Many times just the changing of the placement of a word or the changing of a word will clear up the awkwardness.

If you ask your children to read their work out loud or have someone else read it to them and then to listen to what they're saying, they can catch the awkwardness. Remember that they have to read loud enough to hear their own voices.

1. *Each of you kids will have to bring each day each of the following things: pen, pencil and paper.*

   This should be rewritten to read:

   Each day bring pens, pencils and paper.

2. *The bird flew down near the ground, and having done this, began looking for bugs or worms, because it was easier to see them down low than it had been when it was flying high in the sky.*

There are many problems with that sentence. To get rid of its awkwardness, it could be rewritten to read:

   The bird, looking for food, swooped low.

Keep in mind that the point of your children's writing is for them to give their readers information. The simplest way to do this may be the best way.

CLICHÉ

All children like to use expressions they've heard or read. It makes them feel that they're writing like adult authors. Many times you'll catch expressions that they don't realize have been used so many times before that they no longer are fresh and exciting for their readers:

round as a dollar   *pretty as a picture*   *tall as a tree*   *snapped back to reality*
stopped in his tracks   *stone cold dead*   *flat on his face*   *roared like a lion*
white as a sheet   *graceful as a swan*   *stiff as a board*   *limber as a willow*

Usually the first expressions young writers think of when they write will be clichés. If you think you've heard of an expression before, you might suggest they not use it, but help them think of ways to tell their readers what they want them to know using expressions that are new.

COMMAS

I am including commas because they are often seen as such a problem. Children cannot learn all of the comma rules at once. Some will never learn them all. All writers have some comma placement rules they ignore. One thing that will help your children is to teach them to read their work out loud and to listen to where their voices drop inside sentences. That is where a comma goes. This will work for about 95% of comma placement. This works because commas are needed and used to make clear the meaning in writing. They indicate a pause or a separation of ideas.

Rules: Your children should use commas in the following situations:

1. To separate place names—as in an address, dates, or items in a series
2. To set off introductory or concluding expressions
3. To make clear the parts of a compound sentence
4. To set off transitional or non-restrictive words or expressions in a sentence

Examples:

1. *During the day on May 3, 1989, I began to study.*

I had courses in English, math and geography at a little school in Ann Arbor, Michigan.

The parts of the date should be separated by commas, and the courses in this sentence which come in a list should be separated by commas. Your children have a choice of whether to put a comma before the *and* just prior to the last item on a list.

2. *After the bad showing on the test, Bill felt he had to study more than he had.*

   The introduction—*After the bad showing on the test*—to the central idea of this sentence—*Bill felt he had to study more*—is set off from this central idea by a comma.

3. *Bill went to class to study for the test, and I went to the snack bar to feed the inner beast.*

   There are two complete ideas here: 1) *Bill went to study*; and, 2) *I went to eat*. These two ideas can be joined in a compound (two or more things put together) sentence if there is a conjunction *(and, but, though)* between them and they are separated by a comma. Notice where the comma is placed in the example below.

4. *Bob, who didn't really care, made only five points on the test.*

   The idea of this fourth sentence is that Bob made only five points on the test. The information given that he didn't care is interesting but not essential to the understanding of the main idea of the sentence. The commas indicate that the words between them are not essential to the meaning of the sentence.

COMMA SPLICE

A comma splice is when the two halves of a compound sentence are joined/separated by a comma.

Example: *Bill had to take the test over again, he felt sorry he would miss the party.*

A comma splice can be avoided by writing this sentence in one of the five following ways:

1. *Bill had to take the test over again and felt sorry he would miss the party.*

2. *Bill had to take the test over again; he felt sorry he would miss the party.*

3. *Bill had to take the test over again, and he felt sorry he would miss the party.*

4. *Bill had to take the test over again: he felt sorry he would miss the party.*

5. *Bill had to take the test over again. He felt sorry he would miss the party.*

Notice that the punctuation of each of the above examples gives the reader a different idea about Bill and how he felt.

DIALOGUE STRUCTURE and PUNCTUATION

Dialogue is conversation between two or more people. When shown in writing, it refers to the speech or thoughts of characters.

Rules: Dialogue can occur either in the body of the writing or on a separate line for each new speaker.

Examples:

1. *John took his test paper from the teacher and said to him, "This looks like we'll get to know each other well." The teacher looked surprised and said with a smile, "I hope so."*

2.   *John took his test paper from the teacher and said to him, "This looks like you and I'll get to know each other well."*
   The teacher looked surprised and said with a smile, "I hope so."

3. *John took his test paper from the teacher and thought, "This looks like I'll get to know this old man well this year." The teacher looked surprised—almost as if he had read John's mind—and thought, "I hope so."*

DICTION

Diction is the words chosen—your children's vocabulary as they use it.

Rules: There are at least four levels of diction:
1.   FORMAL: The words of educated people when they are being serious with each
                    other.

   Example: *Our most recent suggestion was the compromise we felt we could make under the present circumstances.*

2.   INFORMAL: Polite conversation of people who are relaxed.

   Example: *We have given you the best offer we could.*

3. COLLOQUIAL: Everyday speech by average people.

   Example: *That was the best we could do.*

4. SLANG: Ways of talking that are never used in writing except in dialogue to show characterization.

   Example: *It's up to you, cook or get outa the kitchen.*

FLOWERY WRITING

Your children will use flowery writing when they want to impress their readers (you) with how many good words they can use to express ideas. This results in the words used becoming more important than the ideas presented.

Rule: A general rule that should apply is: What your children say should be put as simply as possible.

Example: *The red and fiery sun slowly settled into the distant hills like some great, billowing sailing ship sinking beyond the horizon. It cast its pink and violet flags along the tops of the clouds where they waved briefly before this ship of light slid beneath the waves of darkness and cast us all, there on the beach, into night.*

This is so flowery that it is hard to read without laughing. It should be rewritten to read:

We remained on the beach gazing at the darkening sky while the sun set.

MODIFIER (dangling)

This means that there is nothing for the modifier to modify in the sentence.

Examples: *Getting up, my arms felt tired.* (How did the arms get up all by themselves?)

This should read: *When I got up my arms felt tired.*

Coming down the street, my feet wanted to turn into the park. (Again, how did the feet do this?)

This should read: *Coming down the street, I felt as if my feet wanted to turn toward the park.*

Being almost asleep, the accident made me jump. (It is clear the accident could not have been asleep.)

This should read: *I was almost asleep and the accident made me jump.*

PARAGRAPH

A paragraph is a sentence or a group of sentences developing one idea or topic.

Rules: In nonfiction writing, a paragraph consists of a topic sentence which is supported by other sentences giving additional details. A good rule is: A paragraph in this kind of writing should have at least four supportive sentences, making at least five sentences for every paragraph.

Example:

TOPIC SENTENCE: One sentence that introduces the reader to the main idea of the paragraph.

PARAGRAPH DEVELOPMENT: May be made by facts, examples, incidents, comparison, contrast, definition, reasons (in the form of arguments) or by a combination of methods.

PARALLELISM

Parallelism is two or more parts of a single sentence, having equal importance—being structured the same way.

Examples:

1. *We went home to eat and reading.* This should read: *We went home to eat and to read.* This is obvious in such a short sentence, but this is an easy mistake to make when the sentences get complicated.

2. *There are a number of things that a boy must think about when he is planning to take a bike trip. He must think about checking the air pressure in his tires, putting oil on the chain, making sure the batteries in his light are fresh and to make sure his brakes work properly.*

Notice that in this list there is a combination of four parallel participles and one infinitive which cannot be parallel in structure. (This sounds like English-teacher talk.)

What it means is the first three items on the list: (1) *checking*, (2) *putting* (3) *making* are parallel, but the fourth item on the list, (4) *to make*, is not structured the same way, and so this last item is not parallel in structure with the first three items.

This sentence should be rewritten to read: *He must think about checking the air pressure in his tires, putting oil on the chain, making sure the batteries in his light are fresh and making sure his brakes work properly.*

PRONOUN REFERENCE and AGREEMENT

To keep writing from being boring, pronouns are often used instead of nouns.

Rules: It must be clear to the reader which noun the pronoun is replacing. The pronoun must agree in case, gender and number with that noun. The most common error young writers make is with number agreement.

Examples:

Betty and Janet went to the show, but she didn't think it was so good. (It's not clear which girl didn't like the show.)

If a child comes to dinner without clean hands, they must go back to the sink and wash over. (The word *they* refers to "a child" and the number is mixed. This should read: *If children come to dinner without clean hands they should go back. . .)*

Both boys took exams but Bob got a higher score on it. (The pronoun *it* refers to the noun *exams* and the number is mixed here.)

Everybody should go to the show, and they should have their tickets handy. (The problem here is that the word *everybody* is singular and the pronouns *they* and there are plural.) The following words are singular and they need singular verbs: *everybody, anybody, each, someone.*

QUOTATION MARKS

Quotation marks are used to indicate exact words or thoughts and to indicate short works and chapters of long works.

Rule: 1.   Your children should put in quotation marks the direct quotation of a person's words. When they use other marks of punctuation with quotation marks: 1) they should put commas and periods inside the quotation marks; and, 2) put other punctuation marks inside the quotation marks if they are part of the quotation; if they are not part of the quotation, they should put them outside of the quotation marks.

Example: *The salesman said, "This is the gum all the kids are chewing."*

Rule: 2.   Put in quotation marks the titles of chapters, articles, other parts of books or magazines, short poems, short stories and songs.

Example: *In this magazine there were two things I really liked: "The Wind Blows Free" and "Flowers," the poems by the young girl.*

REDUNDANCY

Redundancy means using different words to say the same thing. The writer doesn't gain by this, only confuses and bores the reader.

Examples: *I, myself, feel it is true.*
It is plain and clear to see.
Today, in the world, there is not room for lack of care for the ecology.

This is an easy mistake to make, and it will take conscious thought for your children to avoid this problem. You'll have to help them find redundancies in their work. There are no exercises they can do which will help: just have them use care when they are proofreading their work.

SENTENCE

RUN-ON: This is the combining of two or more sentences as if they were one.

Example: *Bill saw that the fish was too small he put it back in the lake and then put a fresh worm on his hook.* (This sentence needs to be broken into two sentences by putting a period between small and he. It could also be correct with a semicolon between small and he.)

FRAGMENT: This is part of a sentence which lacks a subject or a verb or both.

Check your children's sentences to make sure they have both subjects and verbs.

Some writers use fragments effectively. Your children may do this in their creative writing. They should avoid using fragments in their expository papers.

Examples: Fragments can be powerful if used correctly:

When Janet reached her door she found it was partly open. A burglar! Someone had been in her house and had left the door open.

SENTENCE VARIETY

Young writers have a tendency to structure all or most of their sentences in the same way.

You need to help your children give variety to the structuring of their sentences. A common problem for young writers is that of beginning most sentences with a subject-verb pattern.

Examples: *Janet bought a car. The car was blue. It had a good radio. She liked her car and spent a lot of time in it.*

These sentences could be re-written and combined so they all do not start with a subject and verb.
The car Janet bought was blue. Because she liked it so much, she spent a lot of time in it.

SUBJECT-VERB AGREEMENT (number)

Closely related words have matching forms, and, when the forms match, they agree. Subjects and their verbs agree if they both are singular or both are plural.

Rules: Singular subjects require singular verbs, and plural subjects require plural verbs.

Singular: *car, man, that, she, he, it*

Plural: *cars, men, those, women, they*

Singular: *The heater was good. The heater works well.*

Plural: *The heaters were good. The heaters work well.*

Most nouns form their plural by adding the letter *s*, as in *bats* and *cats*. The clue is the final *s*.

It is just the opposite with most verbs. A verb ending in *s* is usually singular, as in *puts, yells, is* and *was.*

Most verbs not ending in *s* are plural, as in *they put, they yell.* The exceptions are verbs used with *I* and singular *you*: *I put, you put.*

17

Most problems come when there is a phrase or clause between the subject and the verb.

Example: *This red car, which is just one of a whole lot full of cars, is owned by John and Bob.* (It is easy for some young writers to think that cars is the plural subject and write the sentence this way: *This red car, which is just one of a whole lot full of cars, are owned by John and Bob.* The subject of this sentence *This red car* is singular; there are just a lot of words between the subject and the verb, and it confuses the number.)

TENSE ERROR

Tense errors occur when past and present tenses are mixed and there is no justification for changing.

Rules:

1. Present tense is used to describe actions that are taking place at the time of the telling of the event.

   Example: *John is in the house. Mr. Jones lives there.*

2. Past tense is used to describe actions that have already happened.

   Example: *John was in the house. Mr. Jones lived there.*

3. Future tense is used to describe actions that will happen.

   Example: *John will be in the house. Mr. Jones will live there.*

TRANSITIONS

Transitions are bridges from one idea to the next or from one reference to the next or from one section of a paper to the next.

Rule: It will help your children's readers if your children aid them in their reading by bridging their ideas for them. This can be done by:

1. Using linking words like: *however, moreover, thus,* and *because* and phrases like: *on the other hand, in effect,* and *as an example.*

2. Repeating words and phrases used earlier in the writing.

3. Referring to points used previously.

Examples: If your child were to write two paragraphs about pets—a cat and a dog, it would be necessary for your child to make some transition between the two paragraphs—the one about the cat and the one about the dog.

Below is the ending of a paragraph about a cat and the beginning of a paragraph about a dog. The idea of having fun with the cat will serve as a transition to the paragraph about having fun with the dog.

> . . .*and so I get a great deal of pleasure from my cat. She and I have a lot of fun together.*
> *My dog, on the other hand, gives me pleasure and fun of a different nature. We spend time. . .*

VOICE   (passive and active)

Most sentences are built on the order of subject-verb-object. This produces an active voice. If a passive verb is used, it inverts this order and makes it seem as if the object were doing rather than receiving the action of the verb.

Your children's writing will be more forceful if they use an active voice.

Examples:

Active: *Bill threw the ball.   We must spend this money.   Bill drove the car with care.*

Passive: *The ball was thrown by Bill.   This money must be spent by us.   The car was driven with care by Bill.*

Rule: Your children can use a passive voice if:

1. The doer of the action is unknown

2. The action needs to be emphasized

3. The receiver of the action is of more importance than the doer of the action.

Examples:
1. *When we were gone, the house was burglarized.*   (The one who broke in is unknown.)

2. *No matter how hard they played, the game was lost.*   (The game being lost is the most important thing.)

3. *My pet mouse was eaten by that cat.* (The mouse is more important than the cat.)

WRONG WORD

The words your children use do not always mean what they think they do.

Rule:
> Your children should not try and use words in their writing that they don't feel comfortable with in their talking. If they would never say the words *alas* or *to no avail* or *travail* they should not write them.

STUDENT WRITING
WITH
COMMENTS BY PARENTS
AND CONVERSATIONS WITH DAVE

A number of young writers and their parents were kind enough to allow me to use their work as examples of what might be expected of homeschooled children using *Writing Strands* exercises. I have typed the students' work exactly as they wrote it so you could see what their problems and abilities are. I was much encouraged when I read what these students had written. The comments the parents made were valid and it supported my belief that homeschooling parents can do a good job teaching one of the hardest things there is to teach.

Matthew Cross
Grade 2
WS Level 2
Assignment 7

FIRST ROUGH DRAFT

Tom the turkey

This is a story of tTom Turkey, who hid from tThanksgiving 34 days before. ⊖This story starts one day when farmer ∈ Matthew was looking for tTom Turkey to kill him for tThanksgiving day. (farmer mattew wanted tTom for his dinner, because tTom was old and had child/ren.) Tom knew it was close to tThanksgiving day, Bbecouse his father died this time last thanksgiving [*So Tom*] hid 4 days ~~and he was hiding~~ under a brook and waited [*there*] for a long time.
[*paragraph*] ~~and~~ aAfter 4 day's he came out and the farmer said, ["] I'm going to have you for dimner tonight

the End

Mother's comments

What does Tom do and think or say. What does the Farmer do then?
If he doesn't have Tom for dinner what does he have?
Does he still keep trying to kill Tom?

Matt's rough draft continued

[*paragraph*] Tom thought, "I'll sneak a way into the field with my children when farmer matthew goe's in the house and get's his knife."

[*paragraph*] fFarmer mMatthew started to the barn to put his norses in. aAs farmer mMatthew came out of the barn and headed toward the house[,] Tom called his children and ran to the fields. Farmer mMatthew with his knife came out of the house and said, "hHere tTom⁻, tTurkey tTom," but tTom did not come. *as [he]* was running down the road with his chil*[d]*ren in front of him. Farmer Matthew [n]ever saw him again and had had to have chicken instead. thE

This is a wonderful rough draft for second grade! Matt printed it on lined paper and it's easy to see his mind working with all the scratch-outs, erasures, and changes. It shows a good imagination, a clear grasp of the conflict, and has certainly solved Tom's problem.

Matt's mother made some good suggestions to her son about this rough draft and the effect of that help is evident in the final draft. I would suggest that Matt ask his mother go back with him to look at the four things that he would have to decide for this story. They are:

a) Why Tom hid (The reader knows why, but does Tom?) Matt solved some of this problem with the final draft.
b) Where Tom hid (Matt put Tom under a brook) How could this be? Under a bridge?
c) When Tom came out from hiding
d) What the farmer did or thought when he saw Tom after Thanksgiving day

It's important to this exercise that the writer, even at Matt's age, understand that stories have structure and the four suggestions are dealing with that aspect of writing. Matt's mother did deal with these four problems well. She has a right to feel proud of her son's writing at this age and level. Matt has done a wonderful job.

FINAL DRAFT

Tom the Turkey

    This is a story of Tom Turkey, who hid 4 days before Thanksgiving. This story starts one day when Farmer Matthew was looking for Tom Turkey to kill him for Thanksgiving day.
    Farmer Matthew wanted Tom for his dinner, because Tom was old and had children. Tom knew it was close to Thanksgiving day, because his father died this time last Thanksgiving. So, Tom hid 4 days under a brook and waited there for a long time.
    After 4 days he came out and the farmer said, "I'm going to have you for dinner tonight.

"Tom thought, "I'll sneak away into the field with my children when Farmer Matthew goes in the house and gets his knife."

Farmer Matthew started to the barn to put his horses in. As Farmer Matthew came out of the barn and headed toward the house, Tom called his children and ran to the fields. Farmer Matthew with his knife came out of the house and said, "Here Tom, turkey, Tom," but Tom did not come as he was running down the road with his children in front of him. Farmer Matthew never saw him again and had to have chicken instead.

THE END

EVALUATION

Matt has a good visualization of the story setting, and uses it in his telling of the events.

He sets up the problem for Tom and then has Tom solve the problem. He presents his reader with a good understanding of the characters' actions. Matt has done a fine job of writing here.

I wouldn't, at this stage, worry much about some of the details of punctuation, capitalization or paragraphing. I would be too pleased with his ideas and grasp of the conflicts in the story line.

CONVERSATION WITH MATT

I would love to work again with a bright seven-year-old like Matt. I think it's really exciting to watch good young minds work with ideas and express them. Since I don't have access to Matt, I have made up a conversation between Matt and Dave (myself) dealing with his writing of this story. I would say these things and I would imagine Matt might respond in similar ways:

Dave: *Matt, I'm so proud of you. This is just a wonderful story.*

Matt: *I had fun writing it. I especially like thinking about Tom running away with his children when Farmer Matthew came out of the house with his knife.*

Dave: *Could you see in your mind the picture of the farmer with the knife?*

Matt: *Sure.*

Dave: *What did you see?*

Matt: *He had a long knife in his hand.*

23

Dave: *What else did you see?*

Matt: *What do you mean?*

Dave: *It's important that you create the picture you see in your mind in the mind of your reader. To do that, you have to tell your reader what you see in your mind, or in your imagination.*

Matt: *Okay. How do I do that?*

Dave: *What I do when I write is watch the pictures in my mind as if I were watching a movie on TV. Then, when I describe what I see, the reader can see the same pictures. Do you want me to help you learn to do that?*

Matt: *Sure!* (I bet Matt *would* say that at this point.)

Dave: *Even if you didn't see a movie in your head when you wrote the story, you can see one now, working with me. What you have to do is picture in your mind the scene of the farmer coming out of the house with his knife. If you haven't done this before, it might seem hard or strange to you, so, I'll ask you some questions about the scene and you tell me what you see in your mind. If it helps, you might shut your eyes as you think about what you're seeing. Ready?*

Matt: *Yep.*

Dave: *What was the temperature like on Thanksgiving day?*

Matt: *I don't see anything.*

Dave: *That's okay, we haven't started yet. You live in Michigan. It's November 28th. In your state what is the weather like on that day?*

Matt: *It's cold. Sometimes, like this year, it even snows.*

Dave: *Good. If you lived in Georgia, it wouldn't be cold on that date and a farmer living there wouldn't wear the same clothes he would be wearing in your state, would he?*

Matt: *No. Oh, I see what you mean. Okay, the farmer was wearing a coat. . .I see it! It was brown and there were holes in the elbows. He had on a hat with ear flaps, and big boots, rubber ones.*

Dave: *Good! Now run the movie in your head and tell me about the knife. How he held it and what he did with it. What was he looking at? Where did he walk? How did he walk? Was it like he knew where he was going, or did he walk like he was confused?*

Did he go right to the barnyard to call Tom or did he call Tom from his yard? This is what you want to tell your reader in this story. Do you want to tell me now about what you see and I will help you write this description?

Matt: *Sure. Let's see. . .Farmer Matthew came out of his house with a big butcher knife in his right hand. He held it behind his back and it pointed up.*

Dave: *Good touch. He was hiding it from Tom, wasn't he?*

Matt: *Yah, he knew Tom was smart and he didn't want Tom to see what was going to happen. He walked to the barnyard and called, "Here, Tom. Tom Turkey, Tom." He didn't see Tom anywhere. There were other turkeys in the barnyard, but not Tom.*

Dave: *Where was Tom? Now do the same thing. Run the movie in your mind and tell me what you see Tom doing. In your story you say that Tom was running away with his children. Your reader needs to see that. Talk about what the road looked like and how the birds were running away.*

Matt: *There was a gravel road in front of Farmer Matthew's house. There was a corner and Tom and his children were running around the corner headed for a big bird park where they would all be safe.*

Dave: *Excellent. Now, describe how Tom was running and how many children he had and where they were and how they were keeping up with Tom. Were any of them looking back at the farm?*

Matt: *Tom Turkey was in the lead and he was running fast. His five children were right behind him. There was one who was little who was having trouble keeping up. He was about ten feet behind the rest of them, and he kept looking back at the farm like he was afraid he was going to be caught.*

Dave: *What about the steps of the children. Did they have trouble keeping up?*

Matt: *The children had to run and hop and flap their wings to keep up. They were chirping and flapping and hopping down the road.*

Dave: *Wonderful! Now all you have to do is put that in the story and your reader will see the same movie that you see in your mind. I have written down here what you told me. You put it in your story and then tell me if you don't think you like it.*

25

A conversation like this one could only be possible with a parent and child who were used to talking together. Children need to talk *with* their parents. Conversations where they are asked what they think and how they feel. That might make possible this kind of a conversation about writing.

What Matt's visualizing might do to his story:

> As Farmer Matthew came out of the barn and headed toward the house, Tom called to his children. Farmer Matthew came out of his house wearing a coat. It was brown and there were holes in the elbows. He had on a hat with ear flaps, and big boots, rubber ones. He had a long butcher knife in his right hand. It was pointed up and he held it behind his back.
>
> He knew Tom was smart and he didn't want Tom to see what was going to happen. He walked to the barnyard and called, "Here, Tom. Tom Turkey, Tom." He didn't see Tom anywhere. There were other turkeys in the barnyard, but not Tom.
>
> There was a gravel road in front of Farmer Matthew's house. There was a corner and Tom and his children were running around the corner headed for a big bird park where they would all be safe.
>
> Tom Turkey was in the lead and he was running fast. His five children were right behind him. There was one who was little who was having trouble keeping up. He was about ten feet behind the rest of them, and he kept looking back at the farm like he was afraid he was going to be caught. The children had to run and hop and flap their wings to keep up. They were chirping and flapping and hopping down the road. Farmer Matthew never saw Tom again and had to have chicken instead.

If you're thinking that there's a lot of Dave in this invented ending of Matt's story, you'd be right. But, that doesn't matter. What matters is that Matt would have learned something about writing, and not that every word in the story would be his. The time will come when Matt won't let anyone put words in his stories, but for now he needs this kind of experience. So, if you help your children write their stories in this way, that's great. Help them while you can. So soon they'll be gone and you won't be able to help any more. That's sad, but it's got to happen.

Sentence and Paragraph Control

FINAL COPY

The objectives of this exercise are to teach the child how to:
1. Include more than one piece of information in a sentence
2. Understand the relationship between main and supporting ideas
3. Write a paragraph that includes all the information in an organized way.

On days one and two Amanda is to add pieces of information to a core sentence. The point is to teach her that one sentence can have lots of information and how to write a good sentence that has a number of points in it. In this case the core sentence is: *The boy found the dog.* She is to write five sentences adding new information each time. She wrote:

1. *The boy found the dog when he was eleven.*
2. *The boy found the black dog when he was eleven.*
3. *The boy found the black Labrador when he was eleven.*
4. *The eleven year old boy tied the black Labrador with a string after he found him.*
5. *The eleven year old boy found the black Labrador in the park and tied him with a string.*

There are some minor problems with this, but Amanda really understood the exercise and did a perfect job with it. It must not have been too challenging for her. Wonderful job, Amanda.

On days three and four Amanda is to write her own core sentence in present tense and add one additional new piece of information each time in five sentences. Her core sentence is: *The girl flies the kite.* She wrote:

1. *Diana sees the girl fly the kite.*
2. *Diana sees Anne fly the kite.*
3. *Diana sees Anne fly the green kite.*
4. *Diana sees fourteen-year-old Anne fly the green kite.*
5. *Diana sees fourteen-year-old Anne fly the green kite in the sunny weather.*

EVALUATION

Amanda doesn't make *any* mistakes! The organization and construction of a paragraph was no problem for her.

The next part of this assignment: Idea for a paragraph:

She wrote: *Christmas Holiday I enjoyed*

A List of Information I Want to Give:

1. *Being with family*
2. *eating*
3. *presents*
4. *decorations*
5. *playing*

Writing a topic sentence: *When I entered my Grandma's living room, I saw Aunt Mary and knew that I would have fun with her because she was a nice Aunt.*

Listing the information to be included in the support of the topic sentence:

1- *Being with family*
A. *Fun*
B. *Happy to see them*

2- *Eating*
A. *smelled good*
B. *tasted delicous*
C. *made me full*
D. *Turkey*
E. *Ham*
F. *Pie/Cake*

3- *Presents*
A. *How pretty they looked*
B. *How I did not want to open them*
C. *How many there were.*

This listing is good. I might suggest to Amanda that there really is too much information here for just one paragraph. If she were to try and include all of these ideas in one paragraph, she might find that it was much too long. I would suggest to her that she focus on just one major idea for her paragraph. Also, I would show Amanda how to set her listing up in outline form, such as in the example below:

1. *Being with family*
   A. *Fun*
   B. *Happy to see them*

2. *Eating*
   A. *Smelled good*
   B. *Tasted delicous*

28

  C. *Made me full*
  D. *Turkey*
  E. *Ham*

3. *Presents*
  A. *How pretty they looked*
  B. *How I did not want to open them*
  C. *How many there were*

Writing the paragraph using this topic sentence and this listing of information, Amanda wrote the following paragraph:

> *Two years ago I had a great Christmas. When I entered my Grandma's living room, I saw Aunt Mary and knew that I would have fun with her because she was a nice Aunt. The scrumptious food that was set before me on Christmas day was made up of good smelling things such as turkey, ham, pie, and cake, and by the time I was finished I was stuffed. I did not want to open the many presents because they were so pretty. The shining decorations were beautiful and there was even a seven foot high Christmas tree. My cousin Joseph and I went outside to play in the snow with my new sled and it was great fun!*

This is a nice paragraph. I certainly would tell Amanda that she had done a fine job. There is lots of detail here, her tenses are consistent and she has focused her descriptions on that ". . .great Christmas." She has a really good ability to put sentences together. Her sentence: *The scrumptious food that was set before me on Christmas day was made up of good smelling things such as turkey, ham, pie, and cake, and by the time I was finished I was stuffed,* is really nice. She should be proud of this ability. If a child can write one great sentence, the skill is there, and that child can write that well any time there is the motivation to do so.

Amanda, obviously, is ready to write controlled paragraphs. I would suggest the following ideas to her after I had told her how well I thought she'd done:

Amanda, there are some things that you might think about that would make this fine paragraph even better. The topic sentence you constructed to use in this paragraph mentions your aunt and the fun you planned on having with her because she's nice.

That's a good idea for a paragraph, but a topic sentence does limit the things you can talk about in the paragraph. In this case, since you talked about having fun with your Aunt Mary, you should limit your descriptions in the paragraph to the fun you had with your aunt and not talk about anything else. If you want to talk about the good dinner or having fun with Joseph, then you should write other paragraphs about them.

This doesn't make the paragraph you wrote a bad one. I like it. But, for practice, I'd like you to write another paragraph just about having fun with your aunt.

One of the reasons this is such a good job is that the real topic sentence of your paragraph is: Two years ago I had a great Christmas. *With that as a topic sentence, the rest of the paragraph is just about the great time you had at Christmas, and your paragraph is constructed just right.*

There is one very minor thing I want you to know about. The words, aunt *and* cousin, *just like the words* mother *and* grandfather *and* brother *are not capitalized unless the person's given name follows them. For example,* Aunt Mary. *In this case the word aunt is capitalized because it is followed by your aunt's given name. But, when you talk just about your aunt or your grandmother and don't use their given names, you shouldn't capitalize the words.*

Christy
Age 10
Grade 5
Level 3
Assignment four

Description of My Friend

The objectives of this exercise are to:
1. Organize what is described
2. Describe in sentences what a friend looks like
3. Have the paper proof-read
4. Rewrite to improve

A listing of characteristics for looks and actions:

FIRST ROUGH DRAFT

Height - 4ft 1 in.
Weight - 59 pounds
Color - White
eyes - brown
Hair - Blond

Hobbies - LEGOS, WHISTLING GYMNASTICS

Things I like best about this person is He likes almost everything I like. He is fun to play with.

Noah Hall is my best friend. He is homeschooled & is in third grade.
Noah is my brother. We live on Everglade Dr. in Maryland.
He weighs about 59 pounds & is about 4 ft 1 in. tall. His eyes are brown & his hair
is blond. He loves to play with Legos, Whistle, & Do gymnastics. Noah loves to
play outdoors so he is very tan.

SECOND DRAFT

Mother's comments in [ ].

Noah Hall is My very Best friend. We are both homeschooled. I am in fifth
grade [and] He is in third grade.
Noah is my younger brother. We both live on Everglade Dr. in [Salisbury],
Maryland. He is about 4ft.1 & Wieghs almost 60 pounds. His hair is a sandy
blond. He needs haircut. Noah has huge brown eyes. ~~The're really~~ [They're very]
pretty. He really enjoys play[ing] with Legos, Whistling, & practicing gymnnastics.
He likes to play outside, so he is ~~really~~ tan. Noah is 8 years old, his birthday is
August 23th[rd].

FINAL COPY

MY BEST FRIEND

Noah Hall is my very best friend. We are both home schooled. I am in fifth
grade, and he is in third grade. Noah is my younger brother. We both live on
Everglade Drive in Salisbury, Maryland. He is about four foot one, and weighs
almost 60 pounds. His hair is a sandy blond. He needs a haircut. Noah has huge
brown eyes. They're very pretty. He really enjoys playing with Legos, whistling,
and practicing gymnastics. He likes to play outside, so he is tan. Noah is eight
years old; his birthday is August 23rd.

EVALUATION

Christy's mother did a really good job helping Christy with the rough drafts. As you can see, most of the problems encountered in the first and second drafts disappear in the final copy. I wish I had taped the conversations they had about this paper. I feel we could all learn something.

Christy is a great little writer. She has done a good job. I've had ninth graders who couldn't write as well. She is going to be a good user of her language if she keeps up this level of work. With a child who is this good, I would ask that she go back to the assignment and look at the suggestions again. That's what they are, just suggestions, but since they are there, there must be a good reason for them and Christy should look closely at them again. An example of the directions from the assignment will show what I mean:

You should try and use as much detail in your description as you can. It would be good if you were to use examples. When you tell about your friend's eyes, you should do more than just say that they are blue or brown. Tell how your friend uses her eyes. This can read like this:

> *When Janet is thinking, her brown eyes get big and round, and then she half closes them. When this happens, I know she is thinking of something that she likes very much.*

When you tell about your friend's hair you should say more than that it is brown. You should give details about how it is cut and what your friend does with it. This can read like this:

> *John's hair is longer than his mother would like it to be, but John likes it long. He is always pushing it out of his face with his fingers. He has a lot of trouble with it when we play ball.*

At this point I think it might have helped Christy to have a conversation with her that would have been similar to this one:

DISCUSSION WITH CHRISTY

Christy, the directions and their examples say that when you talk about your brother's characteristics, you should give details and examples.
Yes, I saw that, but I don't know what to say.
Let me help, okay?
Sure.
You say that his hair is sandy brown and that he needs a haircut, and that's all you say about it. What about details?
Like what?
What is the shape of his haircut?
It's kinda' like a brush cut.
Sure it is. Good. What about it?
He keeps running his hands over it whenever he's thinking about something. Is that what you mean?
It sure is! That's a good point. Now your reader will be able to see Noah use his body as you talk about what he's like. What about how long it is?
I said he needed a haircut.
How short does he get it cut?
As short as possible 'cause he hates to get a haircut.
Excellent. That should be in there some way.

32

Okay.

Now, when you say he likes playing with Legos, that's all you say. What does he make out of them? When did he get them? How many does he have? What does he like to save once he's made it? Where does he keep them and who plays with them with him? These are all questions you could answer to give your readers details about your brother and let them get to know him. Does that make sense to you?

Sure it does, but that's a lot of work!

Yes, and that's what it's going to take to make you a really good writer. You understand how important that is don't you?

I guess I do, thanks.

An ideal conversation with Christy, but not so far off the mark for most kids who are bright and as eager to learn as she is.

There is no problem with rewriting with your child. You might feel that you're doing your child's work, but that's one of the great points about homeschooling—you don't have to worry about anybody checking up on your child but yourself. If the rewriting is explained and the reasons for change are talked about, if you and your child agree that the rewritten passage is better, and if your child understands what you did to make it better—and this is a must, your child must understand the reasons and process—then the rewriting can only help. If you rewrite for your child, the learning will take place, and the next time writing is assigned that exercise will be remembered. If not, do it again.

Christy has good control of her sentences, and I think she's ready to combine the information in the first four sentences in her paper. They now read:

> *Noah Hall is my very best friend. We are both home schooled. I am in fifth grade, and he is in third grade. Noah is my younger brother.*

Christy could be shown how to combine these pieces of information. After working with her the sentence might read:

> *Even though Noah Hall is my brother and is only in the third grade, and I'm in the fifth grade in homeschooling, he's my best friend.*

That's a lot of information for a fifth grader to get in one sentence. But with this as an example written for Christy, I bet she could do as good a job the next time.

CONVERSATION WITH CHRISTY

It might help you if I made up the kind of conversations Christy and I might have in her attempt to learn how the combining could be done and let you see the process of helping her understand how to combine the first four sentences in her paper.

Christy, the first four sentences act as a kind of introduction to your description. But they read kind of jerky. They're not smooth. I bet if you were to combine the information in them into one sentence, that this introduction would read smoother. Why not try this?
Sure, I can do that.

Noah Hall is my very best friend and we are both homeschooled, I am in the fifth grade and he is in third grade, he is my brother.

That's putting all the information together into what looks like one sentence. Good try, Christy, but there are some problems with that sentence. You have a run-on sentence here. One thing you might try is to rearrange the information so it all fits together and you don't have such an awkward sentence.
Why is it a run-on?

The first two sentences combined create a compound sentence, but, because it is so short, it doesn't need a comma before the conjunction and. *Then the third and fourth sentences are separate sentences just tacked on to the end of the second sentence.*
Okay, I see that. So, how do I rewrite it?
What you have to do is look for the pieces of information you're giving your reader in the four sentences and make a listing of them. (This can be done in your head or you can write them down if that helps.)
I'll write a list of all the information.
Okay.

1. Noah Hall   4. I'm in 5th grade
2. best friend   5. He's in 3rd grade
3. both homeschooled   6. brother

How's that?
Fine. You've got all the information in the four sentences in a listing. The next step is to see which bits of information can go together. Make another list and put those that go together under the same number.

1. Noah Hall, best friend, brother
2. homeschooled, 5th grade, 3rd grade

Good for you. I know, because you put them together, that you can see that there are connections between the items in the two groups.

Sure.

Let's make two sentences out of the two groups and then we'll figure out a way to combine the two groups.

How about this?

Noah Hall is my brother and my best friend. *And for the second one:* I am in the 5th grade and he is in the 3rd grade in our home school.

Excellent! Now you have all six pieces of information in two sentences. That's not bad writing just the way it is, but I'd like you to learn how to combine these two sentences so that you can feed your reader information faster. This will make your writing what we call cleaner.

How about a compound sentence?

Try it.

Noah Hall is my brother and my best friend, I am in the 5th grade and he is in the 3rd grade in our homeschool.

How's that?

Not bad, but you can't combine two complete sentences with just a comma, you know that.

Yeah, I know it. Now what?

Is there anything that you can see that can link the first sentence with the second one? Maybe just the same way the six pieces of information were put into two groups by connections.

Sure. All the pieces are connected together.

How?

Well. . .We live together, we're in the same family, we're both homeschooled and we're in different grades and he's my friend and brother.

Good. Now you might have to rearrange the information in your two sentences so that you can get all this information in one sentence. In other words, if it doesn't keep your sentence from making sense, you can give your reader this information in any order you want to.

What does that mean?

You don't have to tell your reader that Noah is your brother and best friend at the same place.

What would that do?

Can you think of anything unusual about the relationships in your sentence?

No. . . What do you mean?

Okay, why are you telling your readers this information?

I don't know.

Sure you do. You're describing your brother to them. Remember the assignment? The point was to organize your information for your readers.

Yes.

If you can find something in the first sentence that's related to something in the second sentence that would be interesting to your reader, you could combine them.

How related?

What do you think might be seen as unusual about your relationship with Noah?

Oh! He's my best friend.

Good for you. Sure he is. Now, can you use that information to make the connection between the first sentence and the second? You might have to rearrange the bits of information to do this.

Sure. How about this:

Noah Hall, my brother. . .words, words, words,. . .but he's my best friend.

That may be fine, but what about all the words? I see you now have a conjunction between the two sentences. But it will work fine to keep your sentence from being a run on. All you have to do is put a comma there.

Noah Hall, my brother, is in the third grade and I am in the fifth grade in homeschooling, but he is my best friend.

Excellent job. Now, we talked about something unusual in this description about your relationship with your brother. What was that?

That we're best friends.

How can you get the unusual nature of this relationship into this really good sentence?

I know!

Even if Noah Hall is my brother and is in the third grade and I am in the fifth grade in homeschooling, he is still my best friend.

So good! That's a wonderful sentence. See how much better it is than when you had four sentences? They read like they were written for little kids, but this reads like the sentences in the books I read. Boy, am I proud of you.

Thanks.

There is one thing, though.

Oh, no.

Did you think we were done?

No, go ahead and tell me the last thing.

There might be a better word than if *for the beginning of that sentence.*

How about even though?

Fine. Now, what you're saying with that other word—

I thought there was only one!

Right. But this really is the last one. What you're saying with the word still *in the last part of your sentence is that there might have been a time when your brother was not your best friend. You might be able to do away with that word altogether. Why not try it now?*

Okay.

Even though Noah Hall is my brother and is in the third grade and I'm in the fifth grade in homeschooling, he's my best friend.

This may seem to be a lot of work to you for just one sentence. But this is what it takes. You won't have to do this with your child many times before this comes naturally. And even if it is a lot of work and your child doesn't respond this quickly, you still want your child to have this ability to write, and this is the only way that this skill can be developed.

You'll have to work with this style of teaching for a bit before you become comfortable with it. It may seem awkward at first, but the results are so much better than they would be if you were to tell your child what to write and then you let your words be copied.

Erin Kennedy
Grade 5
Level 3

Even little thing count

Once there was a mother toad and her son. Her sons name was Willy. Willy was a rather large toad and was very arfraid of hunters. He had a very sensible mother. She was allways right

One day willy was chasing a ant. When he caught up to it he stepped on it a thought nothing of it.

His mother who had been watching from the window saw him step on the ant, "Willy," she exclaimed. Willy turned his head and looked at her. She looked sad and angry.

Come here said willy's mom, and I will tell you something. Even-she began-little animals matter. "No they don't" said willy "they can't hurt me or scare me" Quiet said his mom. she continued You see if you squished all the ants then the birds would not have any thing to eat so they would die. And if the birds die then the cats would did of hunger. If the cats die the foxes would starve and die then the bears would die out. And, if the bears die out the hunters won't have any thing to hunt but toads! TOADS! exclaimed willy yes toads said mother. From that day on willy never even stepped on a ant or any other bug again

EVALUATION

Erin,

I'm sending you back your original paper and a typed copy of it just as you wrote it. I'm sure you can find many ways to improve your work, but I would like to make some suggestions even though I have already told you it is not the exercise I had asked for.

You've a great idea here. I like your understanding of the food chain and that everything is necessary for the survival of the rest of life. Your dialogue between Willy and his mother is good. They should talk. I would like to see them talk more. It would be a good idea if Willy's mother were to go into some detail about how important even small things are.

It might help your reader to see where these people are. Kitchen? Front room? In the back yard? Put your characters in a place and your reader will be able to see them better. Your logic is good. I think your mother could be more descriptive about each animal's needs.

Characters should use their bodies. Yours don't. I would like to see Willy hold his hands out when he says: "No they don't." His mother could beckon with one hand when she says: "Come here and I will tell you something."

I would like to use this piece as an example in my book. You might, if you have time, rewrite it using my suggestions. Thanks for sending it to me.

DEVELOPMENT IN WRITING ABILITY

The following three papers were written by Benjamin Flagel who was being homeschooled at the time. The first paper was based on an exercise in Level Three when Benjamin was in the seventh grade. The second paper was based on an exercise in Level Four which he did in the first semester of the eighth grade. The third paper was based on Level Five and was written during the second semester of his eighth grade. Benjamin started public school in the ninth grade and was put in advanced English and received A grades for the entire year. I would like to think that using *Writing Strands* for his preparation in writing helped him.

My Room

This exercise is designed to teach that:
1. The world is organized
2. To describe something, its organization must be understood
3. A writer can help the reader understand better by describing things in organized ways

Benjamin was to describe the objects in his room. The first step was listing the objects to be described. He listed:

1.	Door	7.	Bookshelf
2.	Window	8.	carpet
3.	Table	9.	Desk
4.	Closets	10.	Mirror
5.	Bed	11.	Picture
6.	Dresser	12.	Mouse

He then had to place the objects in some order, so that when he described the contents of his room, it would make sense to his reader why he described them in that order. Benjamin reordered his objects. This was done by the objects' size and importance to him: He re-listed the objects:

1.	Bed	7.	Carpet
2.	Closets	8.	table
3.	Dresser	9.	Window
4.	Desk	10.	Picture
5.	Door	11.	Mirror
6.	Bookshelf	12.	Mouse

The next step was for Benjamin to write a description of the objects in his room. There were to be at least three sentences for each item he chose to use on his list.

ROUGH DRAFT

Benjamin's mother's comments are in [ ].

My bed is the big[g]est and one of the most important thi[n]gs i[n]s my room It is not one bed, but actually two bunk beds. My Dad made my bed while [m]Mom made one of the two quilts. I can sleep in either bed - I choose! I have two closets in my room One of which is a game closet where all of the games are stored. The other one is a large walk-in clothes closet. Both are very helpful.

~~The~~ My dresser is made of ~~the same kind~~ [dark] ~~of wood as the bed~~.

It has four drawers and the top is clutterd with pictures of my friends and cousins. My Grandpa and Grandma gave this to me when I was a baby. [spelling]

My desk is dark green and orange. It has one drawer and little compartments on top of it. Dad made this for cChristmas.

I have three doors in my room. They are all made of light colored wood and are also hololow. Two of the doors lead to closets. One leads into my room.

The only bookshelf in my room has five levels. On the bottomost shelf is most of my baseball card collection. The second one up from the bottom has fifty books on it. On the third one up from the bottom are things that clutter ~~in the~~. like my peg game and my Sower series books. My [baseball card] album is on the fourth shelf up from the bottom. On top is my immense rock collections and my four baseball trophies.

My carpet is light green and white. It is shag carpet with few blemishes. Mom says it's the thickest carpet in the whole house.

My night/stand is dark like the dresser and bunkbeds. It has my clock radio on it and my tape recorder. It is next to my bed and against the east wall.

The two windows in my room are each 3[three] feet by four feet. ~~One is on the~~ [The one on the] ~~north wall is in the middle of that wall.~~ The ~~s~~draperies on each wall are white. Each of the widows has a good view.

EVALUATION

It's too bad that I can't show, in the typing, all of Benjamin's work on this rough draft. As you can see from his final copy, he did extensive work on it before he was done. He has done an excellent job with this rough draft. I would have done just what his mother did for him. Lots of compliments and encouragement. Benjamin has no serious problems with using his language at this point. In fact, I think he is really good at it. He has followed directions very well. He has paragraphed with the change in each item in his room. Good job there. He has injected his personality into his paper by having commented about many of the objects, rather than just listing and describing them.

FINAL COPY

MY ROOM

I have a big room. I need it with all my stuff. My bed is the biggest and one of the most important things in my room. It is not one bed, but actually two bunkbeds. My Dad made my bed, while Mom made one of the two quilts. I can sleep in either bed I choose!

I have two closets in my room. One of which is a game closet. The other one is a large walk-in clothes closet. Both are very helpful.

My dresser is made of the same dark wood as the bed. It has four drawers and the top is cluttered with pictures of my friends and cousins. My grandma and grandpa gave it to me when I was a baby.

My desk is dark green and orange. It has one drawer and little compartments on top of it. Dad made this for Christmas.

I have three doors in my room. They are all made of light colored wood and are also hollow. Two of the doors lead to closets. One leads into my room.

The only bookshelf in my room has five levels. The bottommost shelf has most of my baseball card collection. The second one up has fifty books on it. On the third one up from the bottom are things that clutter it like my peg game and my Sower series of books. My baseballcard album is on the fourth shelf. On top is my immense rock collection.

My carpet is light green and white. It is shag carpet with few blemishes. Mom says it's the thickest carpet in the house.

My night stand is dark like the dresser and the bunk beds. It has my clock radio on it and my tape recorder. It is next to my bed up against the east wall.

The two windows in my room are each three feet by four feet. The draperies on each wall are white. Each of the windows has a good view.

I have one picture in my room. It is a picture of Narnia that hangs over my dresser. It is two feet by three feet and has a brown frame. The picture looks nice on the wall. The only mirror in my room sits on the floor in front of the bunkbeds. It is one foot across and two feet high and has a frame like the picture of Narnia. Eventually it will hang on the wall.

My only pet in the room is my mouse, Gizmo. He is brown and wight all over. His cage is a five and a half gallon aquarium. At night i like to listen to him run in his wheel.

I have a great room and I enjoy the privacy in it.

Benjamin typed his final copy, and did a good job of it. I included his few typing mistakes, not to show that he made them, but because that's the way I decided to put this book together—with the students' writing shown just the way they produced it.

Benjamin did an excellent job with this exercise. The point of this work is to teach the young writer to organize his writing so that the reader's mind can be organized as the material is being fed to it. It's easy to follow Benjamin around his room. He has written this so that it reads almost as if he had been shooting film or taking video pictures. An excellent way to describe things. His conversational tone helped me see the objects.

I would suggest to Benjamin that he impose more variety on his sentence structure. He has some, but the following examples will show what I mean. Many of his sentences start with a subject-verb pattern.

> *I have. . .I need. . .My bed is. . .My Dad made. . .I can sleep. . .I have two closets. . .The other one is . . .Both are very helpful. . .My dresser is made of. . .It has four . . .My grandma and grandpa gave it. . . My desk is dark green. . . .*

I'm sure you can recognize the problem, and so would Benjamin if I had had a chance to point it out to him. It will be interesting to see in his later papers if this problem still exists.

If your child has this problem, it will be easy for you to identify it and show how the pattern might be broken. What you must do is explain about the pattern and then show your child how to change the structure of some of the sentences. Most of the subject-verb structures may remain, but there should be some variety. To demonstrate how easy this is, I have rewritten the first few sentences in Benjamin's paper and removed most of the subject-verb pattern.

> *The room where I spend much of my time, my bedroom, is big. I need the room because of all of my stuff. The biggest object is the bed, and it is one of the most important things in my room. It is not one bed but actually two bunkbeds. Making my bed was just one of the nice things my dad has done for me, and something just as nice, Mom made one of the two quilts. This gives me a choice so that I can sleep in either bed I choose.*

Benjamin Flagel
Grade 8
Level 4
Assignment 2

The Main Points

This exercise is designed to teach the student to:
1. Recognize the main points in a story
2. List the main points in the summary of a story

Benjamin has been asked in this assignment to identify the following aspects of a story his mother selected for him:

1. When the story takes place
2. Where the story takes place
3. Who the main characters are (this should include sex, age, kind of person)
4. The problem the main character faces
5. The force that keeps the character from easily solving the problem
6. The climax point
7. The resolution (how it all works out)

Benjamin wrote:

1. 1930's
2. Swamp
3. Skeeter
   kind thoughtful
   boy
   14 or 15
   Jessy
   hardworking
   man 65
4. That Skeeter wanted to keep the dog
5. Self against self
6. When Skeeter gives the dog away
7. Skeeter uses the reward money to buy Jesse false teeth

Benjamin was to write a synopsis:

"Weep No More My Lady" is about Skeeter a kind, thoughtful, teenaged boy. Skeeter is raised in a swamp by Jesse his uncle who is around 65 years old. One night Skeeter and his uncle come outside after hearing a strange crying. The crying comes from a Basenji (a kind of African dog). Skeeter keeps the dog and teaches it how to scare up birds so Skeeter can hunt. Cash comes to the swamp and recognizes the dog as a Basenji, that was lost by a breeder. Skeeter decides what is the right thing to do and gives the breeder the dog. Skeeter uses the reward money to buy his uncle some false teeth.

EVALUATION

That first sentence is a winner! I am not familiar with the story Benjamin read, but I have the feeling I know it from his summary. He has done a good job of finding the main points. He writes well in present tense and maintains it. I am not sure I understand the force against the hero in this story. I think it is the boy's desire to keep the dog to hunt with. I would like to have had that in more detail.

If you point out all the mechanical errors in each paper to your child, it will be overwhelming. In this case, I would show Benjamin the rule for the placement of commas for an appositive. If Benjamin had written: . . .*his uncle Jesse,* or . . .*his Uncle Jesse,* there would have been no need for commas to set off the word *uncle.* But the way it's
written. . .*raised by Jesse, his uncle, who.* . .it needs the commas where I have placed them, and Benjamin should be aware of this rule.

Benjamin Flagel
Grade 8
Level 5
Assignment 15

The Balloon

This exercise is designed to teach:
1. That characters have emotions
2. That characters can be created who act because of their emotions
3. That the student can write a very short story with complicated characters

Benjamin was given a scenario for a story called "The Balloon" and was asked to write the story so that the following questions could be answered by the reader.

1. Why did Betty's father give Betty so many things?
2. Why did the small boy follow the balloon man and then follow Betty's balloon?
3. Why did Betty give the balloon to the small boy?
4. Why didn't Betty tell her father what she had done with her balloon?
5. Did Betty lie?

The characters should talk to each other. They should be seen to move. The reader should see them "think."

The following actions and descriptions were to be included in the story:

1. Betty will have to see the small boy two or three times and recognize that he wants a balloon.

2. Betty and the small boy will have to live in the same "small" world—the world of kids.

3. Betty and the boy must be seen to be alike in some ways.

4. There must be a reason why the boy doesn't buy his own balloon.

5. Betty must be made to think about the boy before she gives him the balloon.

6. The boy and Betty must exchange "looks." They must talk with their eyes.

7. The reader must understand that Betty does not want to lie to her father. She must hesitate before she tells him where the balloon has gone.

ROUGH DRAFT

Together they decided to go to the park.

Betty noticed soon after they got there that a small boy, a lot like herself, was following the balloon man. The boy was dirty and had shaggy clothes. ~~Betty~~ She ~~was~~ pitied the boy who ~~could not~~ [seemed unable to] buy a balloon.

As they walked in the park, Betty and her father talked. Well, her father did the talking. He tried to talk to her about The World Series or the Stock Market. Betty felt sad that her father couldn't talk about things she was interested in.

The small boy was alone and he wanted a balloon. Betty and her father slowly walked to the ice cream stand. They both had chocolate cones.

After getting their ice cream cones, Betty's father asked her if she wanted a balloon. Betty shrugged. She didn't care. Her father bought her the last red balloon. Betty noticed the boy started following her and her father.

When her father stopped to admire the pigeons, Betty turned around to look at the boy. The boy gazed at her and then at the balloon.

Betty slowly put the string of the balloon into the boy's outstretched hand. The boy smiled then walked away. Betty's father turned around and asked where her balloon had gone. Betty hesitated, not really wanting to lie, then looked a the sky and told him it went where all balloons want to go. Betty took her father's hand like she was holding the balloon string and turned to look at the small boy with her balloon.

And so our story ends with Betty and her father going one way and the small boy and the red balloon going the other way.

45

EVALUATION

Benjamin has written a nice rough draft. Many of the elements demanded by the scenario are in place. This is the time when a parent's help is most needed. The following process may be difficult to get used to if you haven't had much experience helping others learn to write, but it's very important.

The scenario of a story is the story's outline. It doesn't have dialogue or the details that will be in the story, but the elements in the scenario dictate what must be in the story.

So that you won't have to keep referring to the text, I will give you the scenario, and then explain how the elements of it have to be incorporated into the story.

Scenario for "The Balloon"

Betty, an eight-year-old girl, is in the park with her father, whom she sees only on the weekends. He is a kind man but he no longer lives with Betty and her mother. When he visits Betty, he always brings her gifts, and when they are together, he keeps offering to buy her things.

One day, on a walk through the park, he buys her a large, red balloon. There is a small boy, poorly dressed, who has been following the balloon man. He watches Betty's father give the balloon to Betty. He then follows Betty and her father, his eyes on her balloon.

While Betty's father is buying ice cream for them, Betty gives her balloon to the small boy. He runs off with it, a big, happy smile on his face. When Betty's father asks her where her balloon went, Betty looks up to the sky and tells her father that it went where all good balloons want to go.

He smiles at her and tells her he will get her another one. They eat their ice cream and walk on into the park.

Working independently of his mother, Benjamin did a fairly good job of following the scenario. There is also the list of questions that would have to be answered by his reader. His story would have to be written, not only following the scenario, but also in a way that would supply the answers to the list of questions.

The first question is: *Why did Betty's father give Betty so many things?*
Benjamin did not give information on this point. The following conversation might have helped Benjamin understand what information or ideas he should have included in his story.

46

CONVERSATION WITH BENJAMIN

Benjamin, did you read the start of the story that was in the text as an example of how to start?

Sure, I did.

It's okay that you didn't copy it. There are things in that suggested start that you haven't included. Why?

What are they?

Let's look at the text again and see what there is there that you've left out.

Betty's father held her hand as they entered the park. He was very tall, and when he came on Sundays to visit her and take her out for the day, he always wore a suit. Betty was dressed up in her best clothes, so they didn't look much like the others in the park. Most of the people had on comfortable clothes and tennis shoes.

Her tall father looked down at her and said, "What would you like to do today, Betty?" He always asked her that question, and Betty never knew what to say.

Do you see anything in this that might answer the first question that asks why Betty's father gave her so much?

No, there's nothing there about him giving her stuff.

You're right, there isn't. Let's look at the words carefully. ". . .when he came on Sundays to visit and take her out for the day. . ." What does this tell you?

He only came to see her on Sunday.

Why?

He didn't live with her.

Why?

He had to work out of town?

But the text says he came to visit her. If he worked out of town during the week, he would still live with her on the weekends or whenever he could get home. He would not be "visiting" when he came to see her.

Oh, I see what you mean. He didn't live with Betty and her mother. Maybe they were divorced and he came to see Betty only on Sundays.

Good for you. Now you have to include that information in your story so that your reader will be able to answer that first question. "Why did her father give her so many things?"

He felt sorry for her?

Maybe.

What else could it be?

Do you think he loved her?

Sure, he was her father.

Would he like to live with her all the time and not just visit on Sunday?

I bet he would.

But if he and Betty's mother were divorced, he wouldn't be able to, would he?
No.
So, if he loves her but he can't live with her, and he can only see her on Sundays, he must feel bad about that, don't you think?
Sure he would, and he would want to make it up to her. Hey! That's why he gives her so much stuff, isn't it?
Right you are. Now your story has to be written so that your reader understands the situation and can answer that first question.

Dealing with a young writer in this way is time consuming, and it was very hard to do this for all the students I had in public school. Fortunately, you have an opportunity to take more time with your child, as I was able to when I worked with mine at home.

I would have liked to work with Benjamin on this story. I feel that by the time he would have been ready to write the final copy he would have had a story that would give the necessary information so the reader could answer the five questions.

In the directions for this exercise there are listed ten actions and descriptions that should be in the story. This listing is designed to give a young writer help. Benjamin did not include those ten actions and descriptions. Was he in too much of a hurry? I would have to ask that question. It is important for a young writer to follow the directions for any writing exercise exactly and completely. In any college or work situation where directions are written, the expectation is that they will be followed exactly. This takes practice. And, at this level of writing, I think that this should be insisted upon.

I don't mean for it to sound like this is so easy that Benjamin's mother should have done it just the way I did. This is not a terribly easy thing to do for your young writer, and it does take practice to lead young minds by questioning. But, this kind of help can be given by almost any homeschooling mother who is willing to talk *with* her child. Most of the school teachers I know think that <u>talking</u> <u>at</u> <u>children</u> <u>is</u> <u>teaching</u>. It's not. It would be easy to just tell Benjamin what information to put in the story or to explain what he had left out. But, by talking *with* him, Benjamin gets the chance to *discover* what he needs to know. That means he has learned to think a little, and is not just writing what he has been told to write.

Each of the questions in the listing should be looked at in this way. If that were to be done, Benjamin would see that his story is very short, incomplete, and does not follow the scenario. He then could incorporate that new information in his second draft. This means that any young writer who has presented a rough draft as good as Benjamin's, but has not included all of the demanded material, should be helped to understand how important it is to do so. This should be done even if each item has to be looked at by both parent and child together. The young writer might find this tiresome but it is necessary.

Benjamin is a good enough writer so that, with this kind of help, he could write a really fine story. And he may have. I never had the chance to see his final copy. I expect he and his mother went through many of the suggestions that I have made here. I'm sure if they did, his story turned out to be really well written.

Most of the homeschooling mothers I have worked with have said plaintively: "I wasn't trained to be an English teacher. I don't know how to tell my child how to write." I have never talked to a mother who didn't know how to talk, and very well at that. Very few of the homeschooling mothers I have talked with have used what is called "bad grammar." If you can talk, you can help your child learn to write.

The directions for this assignment give ten actions and descriptions that should be in the story. I have suggested to the student that: *Your mother may want to read through this list and talk with you about how you can include the items in your story.* This might seem a lot to ask of a mother, but this is not that hard a thing to learn to do.

I am including more imaginary discussion with Benjamin about this exercise because it gives me a good opportunity to show you how you can talk to your child about ideas and how to get these ideas across to a reader. I will continue using Benjamin as our imaginary student.

IMAGINARY CONVERSATION BETWEEN BENJAMIN AND HIS MOM

1. Betty will have to see the small boy two or three times and recognize that he wants a balloon.

Mom: Why do you think it's important that the boy wants the balloon?

   B: 'Cause Betty gives it to him.

Mom: Why does she give it to him?

   B: 'Cause he wants it.

Mom: Good. Sure he wants it. But the point is, how does Betty know that he wants it? The reader has to know that Betty knows the boy wants the balloon.

   B: She sees the boy looking at the balloon.

Mom: Right. But he looks at the trees, the grass and the sidewalk. He doesn't want them. There must be a way that he looks at the balloon that is different. He must look at it so that Betty knows he wants it.

   B: How?

Mom: How do little children look at things that they think are pretty or at things that they want?

B: They stare at them.

Mom: Then that's what you're going to have to make the little boy do.

B: Stare at the balloon? That's all?

Mom: No. Betty has to see him looking at her balloon a number of times. Each time she looks at the little boy, he has to be looking at her balloon. Then your reader will know what the boy wants and that Betty knows what he wants and that's why she gives him the balloon.

2. *Betty and the small boy will have to live in the same "small" world—the world of kids. A world that her father cannot enter.*

Mom: This can be a problem—trying to show that Betty and the boy are in the same "world." What do you suppose that means?

B: That they're both small.

Mom: Sure, that's easy, but how can you show your reader that they have so much in common?

B: I can have the boy look at Betty then up at her father, and then have Betty look at the boy and then up to her father than back at the boy and smile.

Mom: Excellent! What does the looking back and forth do?

B: It shows that they are both the same size.

Mom: Good. Now, how is the reader to know that Betty realizes that they have something in common.

B: That's easy, she smiles because she wants the boy to know that she recognizes that they are alike in some way. When the reader reads that she smiles, the reader'll know that Betty understands this.

Mom: That's good thinking.

3. *Betty and the boy are both small, they are alone (even though she is with her father) and they both want something. The balloon is just a symbol here.*

50

Mom: Do you remember what a symbol is?

B: Sure, it's something real that stands for something that you can't see.

Mom: Can you give me an example?

B: Smoky The Bear is a picture of a bear with a hat on. He stands for taking care of the woods and not starting it on fire.

Mom: How is the balloon a symbol and what does it symbolize?

B: It's one of the things that Betty's dad gives her. A present. It stands for his caring for her.

Mom: That's very good. It sure does. Remember in the scenario it said: . . .*he always brings her gifts,* and this is one of the gifts. What does the balloon symbolize for the boy?

B: The same thing. The boy doesn't have his dad there to buy him good clothes or to take him to the park, and he wants the balloon for the same reason Betty wants her dad to be with her.

4. *There must be a reason why the boy doesn't buy his own balloon. This can be indicated by the clothes he wears.*

Mom: How can you show the reader that the boy doesn't have any money?

B: It says it right there, ". . .*by the clothes he wears.*"

Mom: Describe them.

B: His shoes can be worn out, his pants can be too short, like he outgrew them, and his tee shirt can be too big. Maybe it is his older brother's.

Mom: But the reader has to know this. How will you do that?

B: Betty can see the clothes.

Mom: Then what?

B: She can look at his shoes then at hers.

Mom: That should do it.

5.   *Betty must be made to think about the boy before she gives him the balloon. The reader must see her feel for the boy.*

   B: That one's easy. Betty can examine his clothes then look at her own clothes. She can look at her balloon and then see the boy look up at it. She can see that he watches her lick her ice cream. He could lick his lips.

Mom: You don't need my thinking on that one at all. Good for you.

6.   *The small boy and Betty must exchange "looks." They must talk with their eyes. The boy and Betty must look at each other, then at the balloon Betty is holding by its string.*

   B: We already did part of that one. The boy looks at Betty's clothes, balloon and ice cream, and Betty watches him looking.

Mom: Yes, but it says that they must talk with their eyes. What about that?

   B: How about this: The boy looks at Betty, and Betty sees him looking at her. . .the boy looks up at her balloon. . .Betty sees him looking up and she looks up. . .The boy looks back at her and she sees him looking at her. She licks her ice cream and sees him watching her. . . .she smiles at him. . .he looks back up at the balloon. And so on. Would that do it?

Mom: Boy, would that do it. That's great.

7.   *The reader must understand that Betty does not want to lie to her father. She must hesitate before she tells him where the balloon has gone.*

   B: That's all done already. All I'll have to do is, when her father asks her where her balloon is, she can start to tell him she gave it to the boy, then stop and think it over and then tell him where it went.

Mom: But what about what she tells him?

   B: You mean where it went?

Mom: Sure. Where do all balloons that are on a string want to go?

   B: Up?

Mom: Yes, and her's didn't go up, it went with the boy. Doesn't mean she told a lie to her father?

B: No. They also want to go with kids. And that's where this one went; it went with a kid.

Mom: That should do it.

8.   *Betty, while she licks her ice cream cone, could turn and watch the small boy walk off with her balloon.*

Mom: Why do you suppose that the writer of this exercise would want you to write about that?

B: I don't know.

Mom: Let's look at number nine: *Betty reaches up and holds her father's hand in the same way that she held the string to her balloon.* In order for the reader to understand this one, the reader is going to have to see the boy walk off with the balloon.

B: What does that do?

Mom: Okay, this is a little complicated. The boy holds the balloon in his hand, the string straight up. He is holding the balloon in the same posture that Betty uses when she holds her dad's hand.

B: You mean that the balloon for the boy is the same as Betty's father is to her?

Mom: Sure. You remember the symbol? The balloon to the boy is the same as attention and love from her father are to Betty.

B: That does get hard to think about. Will the reader understand all that?
\
Mom: The reader really will if you write it the right way. You have to remember that Betty has to see the boy holding the balloon like she holds her father's hand. The reader has to see her see this. Then when you get to number ten, it will make sense.

10.   *The reader could see Betty, holding her father's hand, going in one direction, and the boy, holding the balloon by the string, going the other way.*

B: When the reader reads that part will he understand that the balloon is a symbol?

Mom: We can hope so. Some readers surely will.

I know this looks very easy when you read this, but it never goes this well. There are always problems with teaching this way. But, it certainly is exciting watching a young mind grasp ideas. That is so much more important than watching a young mind memorize and spit back what it has "learned."

T. J. Burkett
Grade 6
Level 4
Exercise 11

FIRST ROUGH DRAFT

A Bright Idea

I awoke that day very sleepy. I stumbled out of bed to open the curtains. I knew the bright sun would wake me right up. I tugged at the curtains until they finally opened. Then I noticed that something was wrong. The sun could not be seen!

I could hear people groping around, trying to find their way to their destinations.

A dog barked as it heard a man falling over a garbage can.

Scientists sent space probes to the sun to see what was the matter.

After a few days of studying the sun, they found that it was burnt out and that we would have to provide our own light.

They were open to any suggestions about solving the problem.

Upon hearing this, everyone tried to think of a solution to this catastrophe. They thought, and thought, and thought, until suddenly the world lit up because everybody's light bulbs went on since they all had ideas.

Since then, the world has been a much brighter place because everybody knows that they have to think a lot more to keep light on the world.

EVALUATION

T.J., you've written a good first draft. You have a fine imagination. I especially like the idea of the world being lit by the "idea light bulbs." Good for you. I laughed right out loud when I hit that part. So creative that I could see all the people in the town walking around with lit light bulbs over their heads. It might be a good idea if you were to take your narrative voice on a walk downtown and let him describe the people with the lit bulbs over their heads. You might even have a little fun by having certain people in town with bright 300 watt bulbs and other people (not so smart) with refrigerator bulbs over their heads.

Could you have the people who don't think well at all use white canes? You have to be careful here that you don't make fun of people. When you work with rough drafts, what you first produce is really an outline. This you can use for your work developing the details. This will also make your paragraphs much longer.

I don't see (at this point) any problems with sentences that we have to work with. Some are rough now, but I expect they will smooth out as you work with this piece. I would work on logic.

First paragraph: Good logic work up to the sentence: *"Then I noticed. . ."* Your reader needs to be shown what you could not see. How did you notice that you couldn't see the sun? Could you see anything, and if so how? If you live in the country there would be no street lights, but if you live in town they would be on. It would have been dark as night in your bedroom. Why didn't you turn on the light? How did you know it was daytime? Clock? If you could see the clock there must have been some light, but from where? Your reader must have some logic in the explanation of this impossible situation.

Other than the can falling over, how could you hear people groping? Describe what you heard. There is a rule in writing that says: Don't tell it, show it.

There is a problem with time in the part of your story where a man falls over a garbage can, and in the next paragraph scientists send space probes to the sun. Too soon. If you keep the space probe, you need to talk about what happens between these two events.

You have written a good first draft. In fact it is so neat that it doesn't look like a first draft at all. By the time I have a first draft written it looks like I wrapped my lunch in it.

I'll be anxious to see what you've done with the logic and the details in your second writing. If you have any questions about what I've talked about, I'll be happy to talk with you on the phone. My number is 684-5375. Check with your mom before you call, please.

SECOND ROUGH DRAFT

A Bright Idea

*I ran home from school that day knowing I would have to study hard to pass the big science test on electricity tomorrow. I knew I would have to study **well** into the night.*

*Everything was going **well** [two <u>well's</u>] and I was studying hard until night began to fall. I casually strided [strode] over to turn on the light. I flipped the switch. Nothing. Then I flipped it again. Zilch. I figured that one of the fuses must be broken. Then I stumbled over to the window. I tripped over a chair on the way[,] [check rule for compound sentences] but[,] once I pulled myself up to see out, the whole block was pitch black. I tugged at the window to open it*

and then heard a terrible commotion. A man had stumbled over a garbage can,
then began yelling loudly that he had [a] *cat jump on him. I also heard a car crash*
into the street light[,] *since their headlights didn't work.* [How did you know it was
a streetlight?]

I inferred that there was no electricity in the world since there were no
headlights on cars that went by and I couldn't see any lights outside.

*Suddenly, a **faint** light came from above me. I glanced up and saw a **faint*** [try
small for second faint] *candle above my head. I didn't think much of it at the time*
but used it to light my book for studying.

Once I got studying again, that faint candle turned into a huge strobe light
[Strobe lights blink]. *I rolled down the stairs and tumbled outside. I began yelling*
at people to pay their bills or do their homework, something to get them thinking
and to light the block back up. Next, using what I learned in science, [I] *hooked up*
a special generator to get the radio waves working so I could tell everybody to think
to light the world back up.

*Once the sun rose **again**, everything was back to normal but at night everybody*
*would have to think **again**.*[think of a word other than again, or you could omit the
first again.]

Afterwards, schoolteachers found the light idea useful since they could pull the
blinds down, making the room dark[,] *then seeing* [see] *how much each child*
thought by the light on [over] *their heads!*

COMMENTS FOR T.J.

T.J., what an improvement! You have really changed the readability of your piece. It's much more logical now, and it's much easier for me to see the action. I'd call this a really good job. Good creativity, fun sense of humor, good understanding of the ideas of the assignment, and a really fine application of your imagination to the *What If* problem. I'm sure you can see how much better this draft is—go ahead and be proud of yourself.

Of course, (You knew this was going to happen.) there are some things that you can do to improve it even more.

First, let's look at the suggestions I made last time, with your other paper, about sentence structures. I found subject/verb patterns and suggested you impose some variety. I recognized your efforts here. Good. Here is something you can do to proofread your own work. Read the beginnings of your sentences. (It must be out loud.) You have to read aloud so that you can hear in your ear, not just in your mind, what you've written. I'll do some for you this time and then on your final draft, just before you send it off, you do it again for yourself. Read the following sentence beginnings to yourself, aloud, and see if you can hear any patterns. This means, do you hear anything about the sentences that sounds alike.

1. *I ran home. . .*
2. *I knew I would have to. . .*
3. *Everything was going well. . .*
4. *I casually strided. . .*
5. *I flipped the switch. . .*
6. *Nothing. . .* (Here you break the pattern. GOOD)
7. *Then I flipped it. . .*
8. *Zilch. . .* (broken again the same way)
9. *I figured that one. . .*
10. *Then I stumbled. . .*
11. *I tripped over. . .*
12. *I tugged at. . .*
13. *A man had stumbled. . .*
14. *I also heard. . .*
15. *I inferred that. . .*

It might help you in your future writing if you were to rewrite these sentences to change the structures some. I have done a couple to show you what I mean.

1. That day when the trouble started, I ran home from school knowing I would have to . .

2. Studying well into the night was going be hard to do, but necessary.

3. Structure fine as is.

4. I casually strode to the doorway of my room to flip on the light. (I combined two sentences to throw out some words and also change the structure.)

5. The click was loud in the quiet room but nothing happened.

6. Again—and zilch.

It's important to you and to your development as a writer that you recognize the importance in having a variety of structures. I would like you to do this with each of the sentences in your paper. I feel it will improve your paper and will make you a more interesting person to read in the future.

There still are some small logic problems with what you tell your reader. This is not serious at your level of writing, but I want to bring them to your attention so that you'll be aware of the possibility of logic getting in your reader's way in the future. The use of *tomorrow* implies that it is now *today* and this is only possible if what you are writing is in present tense or if your narrative voice is in the mind of the character. (If that last part doesn't make sense to you, and since we can't have a chance to talk about this, talk to your mother about what this could mean.)

Why was it so dark outside when you were studying in the house? Why wasn't it dark inside, also?

> *Everything was **going well** and I **was studying** hard until night began to fall. I **casually** strided over to turn on the light. I flipped the switch. Nothing. Then I flipped it again. Zilch. I figured that one of the fuses must be broken. Then I **stumbled** over to the window. **I tripped** over a chair . . .*

You might solve this problem by telling your reader that you must have dozed off at your desk, and, upon waking, found it dark, so you groped your way over to the doorway to flip the light on. . .or something like that to take the inconsistency out of what you're saying. You have a faint candle over your head. I don't remember any image of an idea in a cartoon character's mind being given by a candle. It is always with a light bulb. What you've done is not wrong, but it does give your reader the wrong impression. He might feel that the candle was real. I did.

You might set your reader up with the idea that when you found it dark all over town, you really began to be frightened and tried very hard to figure out what was going on. In this way your reader is already seeing you thinking and the association with your thought and the light bulb will be made. There is a problem with the car hitting the pole. Cars run on gas, air and electricity, and if all the electricity is gone, the car couldn't run. I like the idea of the crash. Maybe you could hear noises all over town and think that they might be people calling out to each other, running into things, bikes falling over, dogs barking because of the tension in their owners, and doors slamming as people ran outside.

I don't want you to feel I am being critical with the ideas in your paper. I think you've done a fine job with creativity.

One thing you want to think about before you write final drafts for handing in is that of following directions. This is really important, because, every time in the future when you have directions that you have to follow that are written down, whether at work or in school, they will have to be followed exactly. That's why people write them down, so that others will be able to follow them just that way. One way to do this is to check the directions again and make sure you did each one just before you write the final draft or do the final job.

I would suggest that you go back and look again at the assignment under *WRITING*. There are five parts to an outline that were given to help you organize your thinking. Check number five.

I really like your idea about teachers knowing which kids are thinking by looking for the light bulbs. Wonderful idea. I'm looking forward to reading your finished draft. There's no harm in giving this final draft to your mom and having her check it for spelling and punctuation. I still do this. (I now ask my wife.)

FINAL DRAFT

A Bright Idea

I had a ton of homeschool stuff to do that day the world turned dark. I was studying so hard that I must have dozed off or something.

I woke up very frightened when everything was pitch black. I got out of my chair and groped over to the door by the light switch. The switches' loud click rumbled throughout the silent room. I expected the brilliant bulb to illuminate the dark walls. Very surprised was I when nothing would happen. I tried again only to come to the same conclusion. Something was very wrong.

I struggled over to the window to see if everybody was having the same problem. Obstacles seemed to pop out of nowhere as I tripped and fell over a chair and hit my head on the wall.

I gazed out the window to see absolutely nothing. I could hear dogs barking as their confused owners slammed their doors when they ran out of their houses. I could also hear a cat yowling as it fell out of a crashing garbage can.

As I strained to figure out why everything was so dark, a faint night-light bulb appeared above my head.

When I noticed the little light, I wondered why it was there. I pondered the sight until suddenly a great, blinding floodlight shone above my head. I tumbled down the winding stairs and rolled outside. I began running down the street, yelling at people to pay their bills or do their homework, something to get their light bulbs shining.

Soon, the sun come up and everything went back to normal.

Now that everybody has to think to keep the world lit, I like to walk down the street at night and see the garbage man, with his tiny bulb above his head, and than going into the university and seeing the scientist, with his blinding bulb above his head. Teachers have also benefited from this because they can pull down the blinds in the rooms, making it dark and then seeing how much each child is thinking by the light bulb above their heads.

There are still problems with this writing, but we can't expect perfection. This is about as good as we can expect T.J. to write at this time. We could go over this paper with him again and again, improving it all the time. But while we were doing that, he wouldn't be able to spend the time learning new writing techniques. It's time to move on. T.J. has learned a good deal with this exercise. You can see the improvement in his work from the first draft. There are still some spelling problems and he needs to work with apostrophe rules some, but that can wait till the next paper. I would call this paper done, and well done at that.

COMMENTS I WOULD LIKE TO MAKE TO T.J.

I'm really proud of this final paper on the *What If* problem. T.J., you've done a really fine job. You have taken your mother's and my suggestions and you've really improved your paper. It's much cleaner and the prose is crisper. That comment might not make a lot of sense to you now, but I'm sure you will be hearing more of it as you continue to improve.

What I really like is, I can hear you thinking and learning as I watch your writing improve. You're using your mind, and that's exciting to me. You have a talent for putting your fine imagination into words, and I expect good things from you. You have the ability and from working with your writing, I can see that you have the will to do good work. I'd like to see your next paper. Send it to me, will you?

Student 402
Grade 8
Level 4
Exercise 11

FIRST ROUGH DRAFT

The Mute Day

It was a bright sunny Mon. morning when I woke up jumped out of bed & tried yelling for my mom and noticed I couldn't make any noise. So I tried stomping on the floor to make noise and get her attention—but no noise came and then I tried blowing a whistle and still no noise. What was going on? So then I ran out of my room to find my mom thats when I found her in front of the television watching the local news or reading it in this case for it appeared the newscasters couldn't talk and so they were writing it on paper and holding it up so we could read it. I read:

"It—appears that all over the city no noise can be heard and ono one can make any.

A lot of people were late for work this morning because the alarm clocks couldn 't be heard when they went off. Paper is going off theselves like wild for the only way to conmunicate is to write it down.

Well that's all for now because I'm running out of paper myself. More news later at 6:00 pm. "

Thats when my mom wrote to me we were going to have to get some paper before it was all gone.

So we walked to the store only to find they were out of paper so we went to a different store & then another & another but all the paper had been sold out *of all them. Finally we tried the "PAPER WAREHOUSE" Luckily they had one notebook left and we got it for $20.00 after a long comprimise with the warehouse manager who wanted us to pay $50.00 for it. the comprimise ended up taking 10 sheets of paper!*

Then driving back home I noticed that at the resturant they had put a chalk board so everyone could write their order down.

At the movie theater they had to put up a sign that all they would have was silent movies with the captions to read.

the library was packed because the only thing the kids had to do was read, it no fun playing without sound effects. Ther was a sign in front of the council hall that said the Mayor called for a meeting for anyone who wanted to come so they could figure out what had happened to the sound and what to do about it.   T h e people all decided the only thing that could have happened was the sound effects and sound machine had been unpluged or messed up.

So the mayor, us and all the other people went down to the top secert room to check the michine—it had been unpluged, but who? Nobody knew so the mayor just plugged it in and all the sound came back.

Later on the 6:00 news the reporters told what had happened there was a mouse in the council hall so they got a cat but while the cat was chasing the mouse it unplugged the michine.

Now everyday when I wake up I make sure I can talk and make noise and everyone in town now keeps a ready supply of paper just in case the michine gets unplugged again.

COMMENTS TO 402

Dear 402,

I am calling you 402 because that number was on your paper and there was no other name. Thanks for writing this **fine** first rough draft. You have a great imagination and you use it. You have followed the directions beautifully. You wrote just what I wanted you to. I especially like the way you had the character solve the problems of no noise. Writing everything down is a *good* solution. Of course, the movies would be silent! Funny to have the newscasters write the news and hold it up to be read by the TV audience. Good touch.

I find that many of your sentences start with a subject-verb pattern. Variety in sentence structuring is good. Otherwise your reader will get bored with reading your work and he won't really know why. Examples from page 1:

It was. . .
I couldn't make. . .
So I tried. . .

So then I ran. . .
It read:. . .
It appears. . .
A lot of people were late. . .
Paper is going off. . .

As you can see, all the sentences on the first page are structured the same way. If this doesn't make sense to you, you might talk to your parents about it.

I like the ending, the cat pulling the plug. Nice irony. High-tech society—we keep pets created from wild creatures—they, by accident, destroy our high-tech communications. Nice touch, 402.

You have good movements of people in your work. This is hard to do but you've handled it very well.

I'm proud of your first draft. You've done very well. You'll be able to catch many of your more obvious errors and omissions on the rewrite. I copied your paper just as you wrote it so it would be easier for you to check your work.

Work with your sentence structuring on the second draft. You might also think about talking about the personalities of the characters when you describe what they do to solve the problem of no noise. One question: How does the narrative voice know what happened in the top-secret room? Thanks for letting me work with you.

Amber Cross
Grade 5
Level 5
Assignment #7

The point of this exercise is to teach that it is possible to control the focus or the attention of a reader by the decision about what to describe and how to describe it. The example given is of two descriptions of a fall morning on the edge of a ravine. In the first one, there is a squirrel that the reader must watch. The character is interested in the squirrel. He may be a hunter, and so the reader is made to focus on the actions of the squirrel, much as the character does. In the second one, the same ravine is described. The reader is given a description of the trees and their change in colors as the sun comes up. The point of this is that in both descriptions the narrative voice, through the character's eyes, forces the reader to focus on different things.

In this assignment the objectives are that the writer will learn that:
1. An author controls the feelings of his reader

2. Feelings help a reader understand what the author is saying
3. There are techniques authors use to control feelings
4. These techniques can be used in young writers' work to create feelings in their readers

FIRST ROUGH DRAFT - FIRST HALF OF ASSIGNMENT

"An Author Makes the Reader Feel"

James walked into the library. When he walked in unto the rugs in front of the doorway, he saw a girl he knew coming toward him. "Hi Ann,," he said when she reached him. "What's the hurry?" "I had to give this to you," replied Ann, handing him a note. "It's from Diane." "Thank's," James yelled after her as she rushed off. He opened the letter. It said:

> *Meet me in the*
> *Quiet Corner at 2:00*
> *Diane*
> *P.S. It's important!*

James read it twice to make sure he knew what it said. What was the problem? Were her parents finally getting divorced? "I sure hope not!" thought James out loud. "Diane is my best friend! Well I'll ask her when she comes." James glanced at his watch. 1:30 P.M. Still a half hour. "Well I'll head over there now," he thought. So, he started up the stairs of the large library toward the Quiet Corner. He finally got to the top of the 50 steps. He rested against the rail, then started toward the Quiet Corner. When he got there he heaved himself down unto the couch. He looked up and blinked. . .

COMMENTS BY AMBER'S MOTHER

Amber's mother's comments will be given in [ ]:

[*This is supposed to be an assignment on description - rewrite and add description.*]

This parent's comment was exactly right at this point. This assignment is designed to teach the writer to control the reader's feelings about a place, and to do this there must be details about place.

With first drafts, it doesn't pay to worry about spelling and punctuation or any of the details of composition. All the writer is doing is getting ideas down on paper and trying them out.

What is important, and Amber's mother caught it here, is making sure Amber understands the assignment and is attacking the problem it presents in a way that will assure success.

SECOND ROUGH DRAFT

Mother's comments in [ ].

As the brown-haired boy walked up to the library, he looked [up] at the sky. It felt warm and sunny [on his face] for such a cold fall day.

The sun wasn't quite overhead, so James guessed it was almost mid-morning. He glanced at his watch. He was right. He turned his brown eyes ~~toward~~ back to the library. He gazed at the ~~hum~~ big size of the library. It was made out of red brick. ~~It~~ and was at least 4 stories high. He decided instead of checking out books, he would just walk around and explore the library. As he walked in and stepped on the bright [blue of the] Persian rugs, he saw Ann coming toward him. Ann was a blond[e] girl with blue eyes and a big smile. "Hi, Ann!" he said when she approached him, "What's the hurry?" "I had to give this to you." she replied. "Thanks!" he ~~yelled~~ [Would he yell in a library?] said in a [hushed tone ~~after~~ Ann as she rushed out. He opened the pink card. It said:

> *Meet me in the Quiet*
> *Corner at 2:00*
> *   Diane*

It was from Diane! He thought of seeing his short dark haired friend. "But I wonder what's wrong?" "Are her parents getting divorced after two years of fighting?" He brushed those thoughts aside and started up the dark oak stairs. As he got up the stairs, he looked at the ceiling. It was high, and the window's reached up to it. "How do they clean those things!" he thought. Out loud he said, "Man, this place looks fit for a King, with all the fancy rugs, high windows, and fantastic carving[s]."

After he looked at the ceiling one more time, he started toward the Quiet Corner. The Quiet Corner was about 100 feet away from the stairs on the left. It had two beautiful burgandy couchs, two red rugs, and two pictures of ships. Every week Diane decorated the Quiet Corner in differant pieces of colorful construction paper. James wondered what it would ~~like~~ look like this week. As he started toward it, he looked up at the whitewashed walls. They reached up to the ceiling. [also] As James stopped and looked over it thourghly, he saw how pretty the walls were with rainbows dancing on them from the crystals in the windows. He finally went into the Quiet Corner. As he eased himself back on the cough, he looked up and blinked. Did Diane ever decorate this room!

Mother's comment: *[Very nice—but for final draft change reason Diane is upset.]*

She had put flouresent red leaves and trees on the west wall, flouresent yellow nuts on the north wall, flouresent pink squirrels and raccoons on the east wall and on the south wall beside him, flouresent [green] lovebirds! As he turned back with his face toward the door, he saw a short, nice-looking, dark haired girl rushing toward him. It was Diane! As she reached him she fell into his arms. Then she broke out into tears. "What's wrong?" James asked, concerned. "My parents are getting divorced, and - and I'm going to be left behind!" she answered between sobs. As James tried to sooth his best friend, he thought, "Who will take care of her?" He dicided from now on he was going to be Diane's provider and protecter. He turned back to the sobbing girl and said, "I will take care of you."

FINAL DRAFT - 1ST HALF OF ASSIGNMENT

EVALUATION

Amber has done a very nice job of correcting the mechanical problems in her rough drafts for this finished copy. This is the way this should be done. The young writer should concentrate on ideas in the rough drafts, getting sentences to say what they should, making the writing smooth, throwing out useless words and repetitions, and removing awkward phrases.

DIANE'S PROBLEM

As the brown-haired boy walked up to the library, he looked up at the sky. It felt warm and sunny on his face for such a cold fall day. The sun wasn't quite overhead, so James guessed it was almost mid-morning. He glanced at his watch. He had guessed right. He turned his brown eyes back toward the library. He gazed at the huge size of the library. It was made out of red brick, and was at least four stories high. He decided instead of checking out books, he would just walk around and explore the library. As he walked in and stepped on the bright red of the Persian rugs, he saw Ann coming toward him. Ann was a blonde girl with blue eyes and a big smile. "Hi Ann," he said when she reached him. "What's the hurry?" "I had to give this to you." she replied handing him a card. "Thanks!" James said in a hushed tone as she rushed out. He opened the yellow card. It said:

Meet me in the Quiet
Corner at 2:00
    Diane
P.S. It's important!

It was from Diane! He thought of seeing his short, dark-haired friend. "But what was wrong?" "Are her parents moving away to Africa like they almost did two years ago?" He brushed those thoughts aside and started up the dark oak stairs just ahead of him. As he got up the stairs, he looked up at the ceiling. It was high, and the windows reached up to it. "How do they clean those things!?" he thought. Out loud he said, "Wow! this place looks fit for a king, with all the fancy rugs, high windows, and fantastic carvings!" After a while, he started toward the Quiet Corner. The Quiet Corner was about one hundred feet away from the stairs to James left. It had two beautiful burgandy rugs, two well-worn red rugs, and two pictures of ships at sea. Every week Diane decorated the Quiet Corner in different pieces of construction paper. James wondered what it would look like this week. As he started toward it, he looked up at the whitewashed walls. They reached up to the ceiling also. James stopped and looked over it thoroughly. He saw how pretty the walls were with rainbows dancing on them from the crystalson the windows. He finally went into the Quiet Corner. As he eased himself onto the couch, he looked up and blinked. Had Diane EVER decorated this room! She had put hot red leaves and trees on the wall next to James on his right. And hot yellow nuts and squirrels were in front of him on the north wall, hot pink raccoons and branches on the wall on James left, AND hot green lovebirds and parrots on the wall behind him. As he turned from the (hot) sight, his face toward the door, he saw a short, dark-haired, nice-looking girl coming toward him. It was Diane! When she reached him, she fell into his arms. "What's wrong?" James asked, concerned. "My parents are moving away to Africa with all my family going except my aunt. And I have to stay here because of school!" she answered between sobs. As James tried to comfort his best friend, he thought, "Who is going to take care of her, and he decided right there, that from now on he was going to be Diane's provider and protecter. He turned back to the sobbing girl and said, "I will take care of you."

2ND HALF OF ASSIGNMENT

In this half, Amber should describe the same building, the same library, but this time her focu should be on a different aspect of what the character observes. She has created a different building At this point I would have asked her to go back and read again the examples given in th assignment and asked her to tell me what there was about the two scenes of the ravine that wer different and then would have had her read this rough draft of the second half of this assignmer to me and tell me the same things about it. I think then she might have seen the difference. I have the feeling that Amber's desire to tell the story and create characters and explain their actions have gotten in her way of writing these descriptions.

FIRST ROUGH DRAFT

As the brown-haired boy walked up to the library, he looked up at the sky. It was very cloudy, and very cold. James shivered and turned back to the library. It looked very grumpy this morning. It was made out of red clay brick, [add more details - windows?] and was almost 2 ~~storiesy~~ high. James decided he would explore the library instead of checking out books. He hurried in, and stepped on the very dull red of the rugs. He looked up and saw a not-to-happy looking girl approaching him. It was Ann. She was short, blonde, and had a [confusing] ~~big smile~~ But she had a big frown instead today. "Hi Ann," James said when she reached him, "What's the hurry?" "I had to give this to you," she said roughly. "Thanks!" James said when she rushed out. He opened the gray card. It said:

> *Meet me in the Quiet*
> *Corner at 2:00 P.M.*
> > *Diane*
> *P.S. It's important!*

It was from Diane! James thought of seeing his dark-haired friend, "But what's wrong?" "Are her parents moving away to Africa like they almost did 2 years ago?" He brushed those thoughts aside [why] and started up the gloomy stairs. As he reached the top, he looked at the ceiling. It was low, and the windows barely reached it. He thought "Man, this place looks like a beggar house, with all the dirt caked on the windows, scratched floors and very-worn rugs." After a while, he started toward the Quiet Corner.

SECOND ROUGH DRAFT

As the brown-haired boy walked up to the library, he looked up at the sky. It was very cloudy, and <u>very</u> cold. James shivered and turned back to the library. James had always thought the library had [too wordy] ~~always~~ looked grumpy, and this morning it looked grumpier than ever. It was made out of red clay bricks. It also had narrow slits for windows that looked forbidden. James shivered again, but not because of the cold. There was something mysterious about this place. [sent a shiver down his back] And he didn't like it. He hurried in and stepped on the bare, unwashed plank floor of the library. When he looked up, he saw the only [only] librarian in the library. She had short, unruly hair very long nails, and a very grumpy attitude. [What makes you assume

67

this?] It was When he asked where his friend, Ann, was she answered very [Use another word] grumply sourly. "Can't you see? She's right behind you!" James turned around so suddenly, he knocked Ann over. As he helped her up he admired her blonde hair blue eyes, but not her big frown. She said meanly, "Well that's a nice help, and how do you do!" "Sorry!" James said, kinda feeling grumpy her himself. Ann stuck out her tongue at him and walked out the door dropping a note as she did. James picked up the note. It read:

> *James,*
> *Help! come to the*
> *Quiet Corner!*
> *   Diane*

It was from Diane! "But what was wrong?" "Were her parents moving to Africa like they almost did two years ago?" He brushed his those thoughts aside, and started up the rough plank stairs. When he got to the top, he looked at the ceiling. It was painted dark brown and the windows reached up to the low was low. The windows barely reached up to it. After au while he went toward the libra Quiet Corner.

The Quiet Corner was about 50 feet away from the stairs. As James headed toward it, he stopped and looked at the ugly walls. They were as high as 7 feet, barely taller than James. It They were unpainted, and had gray streaks on it from the leaking roof. Ugh! I When James walked in, he knew right away who had decorated it. It was ugly! He was sure that the librarian had decorated it. It had gray spiders on the north wall, in front of him. On his right it had black cats on the wall, on his left, there were dull red brooms, and on the south wall there were an ugly witch. It sounded just like the librarian! As he turned around, he saw a short dark-haired girl in tears rushing toward him. It was Diane! As she reached him, she fell onto the floor. James helped her up, and held her. Then he asked, "What's wrong?" she then started sobbing. Finally, she calmed down long enough to tell him her story. "My family is all moving away to Africa except me. I'm staying here with the librarian and am not getting any pay!" James decided right then and there that he would be Diane's provider and protecter from now on. He turned back to the sobbing girl and said, " I will take care of you."

FINAL DRAFT - SECOND HALF OF ASSIGNMENT

Diane's Problem

As the brown-haired boy walked up to the library, he looked up at the sky. It was very cloudy, and very cold. James shivered and turned back toward the library. James had always thought the library looked grumpy, and this morning it looked even grumpier. It was made out of red clay brick. It also had narrow slits for windows that looked forbidden. James shivered again, but not because of the cold. There was something mysterious about this place that sent a shiver down his back. And he DID NOT like it. He hurried in and stepped on the bare, unwashed plank floor of the library. When he looked up, he saw the librarian. She had short, unruly hair, very long nails, and a very grumpy attitude. It was the way she looked and spoke that made her seem grumpy. When he asked where his friend, Anne was, She answered sourly, "Can't you see? She's right behind you!" James turned around so suddenly, he knocked Anne over! As he helped her up, she said meanly, "Well THAT'S a nice hello, and a how do you do!" "Sorry!" James said, kind of feeling grumpy himself. Anne stuck out her tongue at him, and stormed out the door, dropping a note as she did. James picked up the note. It read:

> *James,*
> *Help! come to the*
> *Quiet Corner!*
> *   Diane*

It was from Diane! "But what was wrong?" "Were her parents moving away to Africa, like they almost did two years ago?" He brushed those thoughts aside, and started up the rough wood stairs just ahead of him. When he got to the top, he looked at the ceiling. It was painted dark brown, and was low. The windows barely reached up to it. After a while, he went toward the Quiet Corner. The Quiet Corner was about 50 feet away from the stairs. As James headed toward it, he stopped and looked at the ugly walls. They were as high as 7 feet, barely taller than James. They were unpainted, and had gray streaks on it from the leaking roof. Ugh! When James walked in, he knew right away who had decorated the room. It was ugly! He was sure the librarian had decorated it. It had gray spiders on the north wall, in front of him. On his right, it had black cats on the wall, on his left, it had dull red brooms, and behind him was a very ugly witch. It sounded just like the librarian! As he turned around, he saw a short, dark-haired girl in tears rushing toward him. It was Diane! As she reached him, she fell onto the floor. James helped her up, and held her. Then he asked, "What's wrong?" she then started sobbing. Finally, she calmed down long enough to tell her story. "My parents, and family, are moving away to Africa except me I'm staying here with the librarian, and am not going to get any pay!" James decided right then and there that he would be Diane's provider and protecter from now on. He turned back to the sobbing girl and said, "I will take care of you."

EVALUATION

Amber has done a fine job with this writing. The two descriptions are clearly different. Yet there is some question in my mind about what feelings she wants the reader to focus on in each piece. It may be that Amber's desire to tell a story, which is not part of the assignment, gets in the way of her doing exactly as the directions suggest. The point of this exercise is to have the writer produce two descriptions of the same place, but to describe different aspects of the place so as to have the reader focus on that aspect described in each scene.

This problem is fairly common among young writers who like to write. There is some reluctance to follow only the dictates of the assignments. They like to embellish the work with their own ideas. This isn't bad. I usually encourage this, but only as long as the points of the assignments are met. In the first piece, the feeling I get is that the library is a nice place to visit. In the second piece I get the feeling that the building is not inviting, much like the librarian. This gives me two different feelings, but I am in doubt about what I am supposed to focus on and why. This is a fairly sophisticated demand on a person this young writing at this level, and I might have trouble getting this idea across to Amber. Amber has worked her way through levels three and four, but still, this level five is challenging for a fifth grader. Level five is usually used by first time users of *Writing Strands* who are in the ninth grade or about 15 years old.

Because of this writer's obvious interest in writing and ability to use language, I would make detailed suggestions about improvement. Not as a way to criticize what Amber has written, but as a way to show her how to improve her work. Amber has worked hard and rewritten well using her mother's comments. She should be proud of her work.

I will do this as if I had the chance to talk directly with Amber. I wish I could.

COMMENTS TO AMBER

Amber, you have a good feeling about words and what they can do. I like your flow of ideas. I get the feeling that you like to read. I can see that in the way you describe things and your sentence constructions. This sentence is an example of what I mean: *He hurried in and stepped on the bare, unwashed plank floor of the library.* That's nice, Amber.

One thing you should watch for is the ability of your reader to understand the information you're presenting. You are good enough at writing to be dealing with young adults as your audience. They will be able to understand situations better than you've given them credit for in this piece. An example of what I'm talking about is in the second half of the assignment after the note to James:

> *After a while, he went toward the Quiet Corner. The Quiet Corner was about 50 feet away from the stairs. As James headed toward it, he stopped and looked*

at the ugly walls. They were as high as 7 feet, barely taller than James. They were unpainted, and had gray streaks on it from the leaking roof. Ugh! When James walked in, he knew right away who had decorated the room. It was ugly! He was sure the librarian had decorated it.

You might think about cutting out some of the words in the first two sentences so as to feed this information to your readers quicker. Think about it this way:

The Quiet Corner was about 50 feet to the left at the top of the stairs.

I've combined the first two sentences and so was able to throw away the repeated words, *the Quiet Corner.* You say that, "*. . .he went toward the. . .*" and in the next sentence you say, "*As James headed toward it. . .*" What is happening here is that you're telling your readers two times that James heads toward the Quiet Corner. Your readers may not need the repetition. If you read your work with this idea in mind you'll find many places where you can cut words and phrases out and feed your readers what you want them to know more efficiently.

Another thing you might think about to make this really nice piece of writing even better is in the directions you are giving your readers about how to understand the order of the events as they happen. As an example of this, you've written:

As he turned around, he saw a short, dark-haired girl in tears rushing toward him. It was Diane! As she reached him, she fell onto the floor. James helped her up, and held her. Then he asked, "What's wrong?" She then started sobbing.

Notice that you say, "**As he** turned. . . **As she** reached him. . . **Then he** asked. . . **She then** started. . . "

Stories and books written for young readers have such directions. Children need to be told the order of the events. They need to know that first one thing happens and then the next thing happens and then the next, and so on. Your readers don't need that. They'll be adult enough to understand, without being told, cause and effect relationships, logical sequencing of actions, and, that, in narration, chronological sequencing is standard unless the readers are told in some way that the chronology is being broken.

In this case, in your writing, your reader may not need so many directions. If you decide that they might not be necessary, you could rephrase your work like this:

Turning, he saw a short, dark-haired girl in tears rushing toward him. It was Diane! She fell sobbing to the floor at his feet. He helped her up, held her and asked, "What's wrong?"

Amber, notice that the same information is in the rewritten section, but that the directions to your reader have been left out.

Two final observations. One, you might check the rules for dialogue. An easy way to do this is to look at any novel and see how the author has set up the dialogue. These rules are pretty standard and most writers follow them. An example of this from the first half of the assignment:

> *"Hi Ann," he said when she reached him. "What's*
> *the hurry?" "I had to give this to you." she*
> *replied handing him a card. "Thanks!" James*
> *said in a hushed tone as she rushed out.*

Dialogue should be set up this way:

> *"Hi, Anne," he said when she reached him.*
> *"What's the hurry?"*
> *"I had to give this to you," she replied,*
> *handing him a card.*
> *"Thanks!" James said in a hushed tone as*
> *she rushed out.*

Notice that each speaker starts a new paragraph. This is done so that the readers will be sure who says what.

The second observation: If you were to write a very long story, 20 or 30 pages long, and were to use one exclamation point (!) in the whole story it would be enough! Your writing will be better if you avoid using that mark and construct your work so that what you say will convey the importance rather that ask the mark to do it. Notice in the example below:

> "Can't you see? She's right behind you[!]" James turned around so suddenly, he knocked Anne over[!] As he helped her up, she said meanly, "Well THAT'S a nice hello, and a how do you do[!]" "Sorry[!]" James said, kind of feeling grumpy himself. Anne stuck out her tongue at him, and stormed out the door, dropping a note as she did. James picked up the note. It read[!]: *[The exclamation points are fine in the note. This is the way we write notes.]*

> *James,*
> *Help! come to the*
> *Quiet Corner!*
> *Diane*

> *It was from Diane[!]*

Amber, I'm really proud of your writing on this exercise. You've done a super job, and these comments are not meant to tell you that you haven't, but to give you some directions for maybe improving your writing. On your next piece, try and use these suggestions and see if you like the results.

I am rewriting one of your paragraphs to demonstrate some of the suggestions that I think might help your writing. My rewriting will not be the perfect prose it should be, but if you see that the changes I make might help you, then the effort is worth it.

I rewrote the long paragraph just after the note in the final draft of the first half of the assignment. This will help you if you compare what I have done with your original copy of the same paragraph and try and figure out why I made the changes I did. If you can use the same principles in your work as I used in the rewriting, it might help you. You will better understand what I've done if you put a copy of your paragraph next to my rewriting of it. You should use the copy at the bottom of the next page. The one that is uninterrupted by my comments.

The reader has just read the note and knows that it is from Diane. No need to tell the reader this.

> *He thought of his short, dark-haired friend and wondered what could be wrong. Could her parents be moving to Africa again? He shook his head and started up the dark oak stairs.*

There is no need for quotation marks for his thoughts. Your reader will understand that the words belong in his head. You tell your reader two times that he walked up the stairs, once is enough.

> *As he neared the landing he noticed how high the ceilings were, but that the windows reached from the first floor almost to the ceilings on the second. How do they clean these things, he thought, and out loud said, "Wow, this place looks fit for a king with all the fancy rugs, high windows, and fantastic carvings."*

Now you can use quotation marks because he's speaking out loud.

> *The Quiet Corner was on the second floor almost 100 feet to James' left. The floor was covered with two well-worn red rugs, and there were two beautiful burgundy couches. There were pictures of ships at sea.*

I was able to throw out some words I thought your reader wouldn't need.

> *Every week Diane decorated the Quiet Corner with construction paper cut-outs and he wondered what it would look like this week.*

I was able to combine two sentences into one so as to feed your reader this information more quickly.

> *The white walls, reaching to the ceiling always had danced with rainbows cast from the crystals hanging in front of the windows. But, when he eased himself onto the couch, he had to blink. Had Diane ever decorated this room this week.*

It might help you to actually act out the actions of your characters when you write about what they do. In this case, you have James stop and look over the white walls thoroughly but go into the Quiet Corner and not notice the walls until he sits down. If you were to "walk" through these actions you might see that James would notice the walls in the Quiet Corner as soon as he enters it.

> *She had put hot red leaves and trees on the wall to the right, hot yellow nuts and squirrels on the wall in front of him, hot pink raccoons and branches on the left and hot green lovebirds and parrots on the wall behind him.*

Again I was able to use fewer words but give the same information.

> *When he turned to the door, he saw his short, dark-haired friend, Diane, coming toward him. She fell weakly into his arms.*

The Quiet room would not be so big that he wouldn't be able to recognize Diane as soon he saw her. So, I combined those sentences.

> *"What's wrong?" James asked, a frown of concern on his face.*
> *"My parents are moving to Africa with all of the rest of my family except my aunt. And I have to stay here because of school," she sobbed.*
> *As James patted her back to comfort her, he thought, Who is going to take care of her? And he decided right there, that from then on he would going to be Diane's provider and protector. He looked down at the sobbing girl and said, "I will take care of you."*

You have James trying to comfort Diane while she is crying in his arms, and then you say: "He turned back to the sobbing girl and. . ." Why and when did he turn away from her? These problems can be avoided if you, at least in your mind, act out the actions of your characters.

THE PARAGRAPH REWRITTEN

He thought of his short, dark-haired friend and wondered what could be wrong. Could her parents be moving to Africa again? He shook his head and started up the dark oak stairs.

As he neared the landing he noticed how high the ceilings were, but that the windows reached from the first floor almost to the ceilings on the second. How do they clean these things, he thought, and out loud said, "Wow, this place looks fit for a king with all the fancy rugs, high windows, and fantastic carvings."

The Quiet Corner was on the second floor, almost 100 feet to James' left. The floor was covered with two well-worn red rugs, and there were two beautiful burgundy couches. There were pictures of ships at sea.

Every week Diane decorated the Quiet Corner with construction paper cut-outs, and he wondered what it would look like this week. The white walls, reaching to the ceiling, always had danced with rainbows cast from the crystals hanging in front of the windows, But, when he eased himself onto the couch, he had to blink. Had Diane ever decorated this room this week.

She had put hot red leaves and trees on the wall to the right, hot yellow nuts and squirrels on the wall in front of him, hot pink raccoons and branches on the left and green lovebirds and parrots on the wall behind him.

When he turned to the door, he saw his short, dark-haired friend, Diane, coming toward him. She fell weakly into his arms.

"What's wrong?" James asked, a frown of concern on his face.

"My parents are moving to Africa with all of the rest of my family except my aunt. And I have to stay here because of school," she sobbed.

As James patted her back to comfort her, he thought, Who is going to take care of her? And He decided right there, that from then on he would be Diane's provider and protector. He looked down at the sobbing girl and said, "I will take care of you."

A general comment:

In creative writing there are no set rules for paragraphing, but there are some conventions that may be good to follow. It is usual to paragraph, other than for each new speaker in dialogue, each time there are changes in the following: characters, times, places, attitudes, actions, emotions, movements, or when the paragraph has become long enough so that the writer wants to give the reader a break. You might want to check this rewriting of your passage and see if you can figure out why I paragraphed it in each instance as I did.

USING WRITING STRANDS SKILLS IN OTHER SUBJECTS

The following report was included to give you an example of what a young writer, who has an interest in writing, might produce if given encouragement and training. I don't have the rough drafts for this piece, but after examining it, I'm sure you'll agree with me that there has been considerable work done by this bright young writer. The parents should be proud of Chris's ability to use his language so effectively. This paper was not sent in response to my request to have work sent to me that had been generated by homeschooled children using *Writing Strands*. We found this story tucked in a drawer with the note from Mrs. Walker. She had told us that her children were doing well and we asked to see some of their work.

This paper is not based on a particular assignment in Level 3, rather it is based on Chris's interest in this aspect of his study of American history. Chris has employed what he has learned from his work with specific aspects of his training in *Writing Strands* and incorporated that learning in his other work in homeschooling. Chris has given me permission to include this as an example of student writing influenced by an organized program of training in language use.

Dear Mr. Marks,

You probably do not remember me. I spoke with you at the NYS LEAH convention at Albany, NY in April.
We used the WRITING STRANDS level 3 book and the READING STRANDS book this year. The enclosed story is a result.

Cherie Walker

Chris Walker
Level 3
age 13

Historical Fiction Story Surrounding the Pony Express

July 15, 1860

Dear Michael,

Many things have been happening to me this spring. I just turned 17 last February. A man named Mr. William Russel, a business man from Missouri wanted to establish an express mail service between St. Joseph, Missouri and Sacramento, California. As we happened to live on the Pony Express route our home has become one of the stations.

At first it was my job to care for the horses in the barn. The rider would get a fresh horse from our station and I had to care for the tired, lathered, and thirsty horse he had been riding. I loved the excitement when the rider galloped into our yard and I had two minutes to get another horse ready while he would get a drink of water and possibly a bite to eat.

One day in the middle June, Mr. Russel told me one of his riders had broken a leg. He asked me if I would take this injured rider's place. Mr Russel told me I would get paid 100 dollars a month and would have to ride about 75 miles a day, stopping every 10-15 miles to change horses. I told him I would talk to my parents and get back to him in a couple days.

The next day I spoke with my parents and we decided that I would try it out. I rode to Mr. Russel's office and signed up. He showed me a map, told me the route I would be taking, and told me to be ready the next morning. Very early the next morning I saddled up a horse, got a flask of water, and waited for the night rider to pull in so I could get started. Soon he arrived and gave me the mail pouch. This bag is a specially designed leather saddle bag that sits on the saddle. My weight is the only thing that holds it in place. I jumped on my horse. As I galloped away I started thinking about the perils I might encounter; Indians, thunderstorms, robbers, rivers, and mountains.

After about an hour of riding through the foothills, I heard some yells. When I looked behind me I saw some young Indians chasing me on foot. "Boy, can they run fast!" I thought as I galloped as fast as I could. Shortly I was able to lose them but I was so scared I didn't stop galloping for about twenty minutes. Soon I got to a transfer station on the edge of the Rockies. I delivered some of the mail I carried, picked up some more, and got a fresh horse. A guy named Old Tom lives at this transfer station. I told him about my brush with the Indians. He said that I may have interrupted their hunting party. After a quick lunch I took off again.

Soon I got to a river. It was too deep for my horse to wade across. As I was looking for a shallow spot a thunderstorm began to form. I decided I would have to swim across on my horse. "I hope this horse can hold me," I thought. Finally I got to the other side and just in time. The river started to turn into a torrent and the rain was beating down on me like nails. I started to gallop as fast as I could hoping I could get to the next transfer station before it got much worse. The rain got so bad I couldn't see ahead of me. I was forced to stop under an overhanging rock for shelter. "Thank God for this rock," I said out loud. After about ten minutes the storm let up but the path was so muddy that I had to walk up the hill to find some firm ground. After about half an hour I arrived cold, wet, and hungry at another transfer station.

Mrs. Evans had a nice warm fire going. She had some extra clothes on hand for the riders. I found some that fit, a bit on the big side but they would do. I quickly ate a bowl of her delicious stew and had to get back to work. Next I had to ride through a pass in the Rocky Mountains. It got a little rough but I managed to get through in one piece. In some spots the trail would disappear and I would have to find it again. My last stop was in the Rockies and I got there after about a half an hour. I handed the mail bag over to the next rider and went inside to sleep. I felt like I would fall asleep before I reached the bunk.

I have gradually gained experience in delivering the mail and I can dow do it much better. I love riding for the Pony-Express. I earn good money and have made lots of friends. Write soon.

Your Cousin,

John

COMMENT ON CHRIS'S WORK

Not having the rough drafts of Chris's work or knowing what the original assignment was, it's not possible to know what problems he overcame or how well he did with this nice exercise.

You can't make a reasonable evaluation of your children's writing at any point if you haven't established what you intended for them to learn at that time. This is why each of the exercises in *Writing Strands* has such a clearly defined set of objectives for each exercise. Those are the things you should be looking for in the final copies of your children's work.

If an objective of an assignment is that the child will learn to change tenses when a character speaks in a piece of fiction, that's what you should look for. And it won't be hard to find it if your child has understood the exercise. It should be obvious in the writing that the child has understood and employed that understanding.

Of course, you can look for other things at the same time. That is why there's a page following each assignment in the *Writing Strands* books where you can record the problems your child has encountered. These you can work with one at a time.

As long as you do this as a way to show your child how to make the writing even better, there'll be no harm done to your child's writing ego by offering suggestions. (Note the word used was *suggestions* not *criticisms*.)

If I had had a chance to talk to Chris about this final copy of his paper at the time he had written it, I would have given him high praise. I think he's done a wonderful job. But, suppose he had not written so well. He would still need those people he trusts to help him by telling him that they think he is doing well. He, like everyone else, needs to feel good about his efforts.

The majority of us don't have children who will be professional writers, and to expect perfection from your children, when they're still learning the rules of communication, is too much for them to handle. What is important is that they are working on a writing training program in which you, as parent and teacher, have confidence. What's important is your knowledge that your children are continuing to improve in a series of steps that will lead to the kind of writing skills that will make them comfortable with their abilities when those skills will be called upon.

The point of teaching our children is not to have perfect children, but to have children who are continuing to improve in their abilities and who enjoy both the improvement and the learning.

When we say that finally we are educated, we are saying we have stopped growing and learning and improving and we are intellectually dead. The importance of understanding this idea is that it allows you to accept that the process of evaluation is making sure that your children are progressing, and not that they have arrived. They are not perfect, as we were not and are not, but they are improving; they are wonderful at what they are learning to do, but there is a great deal that they can learn that will help them to make themselves even more wonderful.

What a gift we have to be able to teach our children at home and to watch them learn and develop and not have to trust strangers to care for them as we can. Many times I wish I could do it all over again, I loved it so.

APPENDIX

RULES FOR DRAFTING

There are no set rules for writing drafts of papers. Those of us who have chosen to teach young people to write have to make them up. That's okay. The point of our training is to make those we love and work with competent users of their language.

I can give you the rules I have used for years. They have proven to be a practical guide for my students and have been accepted at universities all over the country.

The *Writing Strands* program was designed to prepare young people to write well, whether they were planning on college or not. I have intentionally omitted some practices which are conventional, but for good reasons. The writing of journals is very common for homeschoolers. If your children have been writing them and like to do so, that's fine. It won't hurt them. In a practical sense, it won't do them much good either. Journals are useful for two situations: professional writers use them to record scenes, characters, situations, experiences or thoughts that they want to save for future use. And professionals use journal writing to break out of writing blocks. They force themselves to write every day in a journal until the words flow smoothly again.

Most teachers who teach journal writing do so because it's easy and the kids produce lots of paper, and they think that they're teaching the kids to write. Most proponents of journal writing suggest that the journals not be corrected. The students should not feel inhibited by the pressures of form. So, what are they learning about writing? They're really just reinforcing their errors week after week. They're learning nothing about techniques of communication. They might as well be copying words out of some novel and calling that writing training. In fact, in many schools, that's what the kids do, they copy page after page and turn them in. Since it isn't graded or corrected, who cares?

In order to learn to communicate, students need to have goals, an audience, and a person more adept than they are at word use who can look at their efforts and advise ways to improve them. That is where drafting comes in.

If we give students writing assignments, collect them, write comments on them, grade them and return them, the students will learn nothing about writing. Unfortunately this is what is done by most English teachers, usually because they don't feel they have time to really teach writing. If writing training is carried on this way, the students write on the second paper the same way they wrote on the first. They might look at the corrections the teacher's made on the first paper, but that's all. They'll continue to make the same errors and will have no opportunity to develop the writing skills they so desperately need.

FIRST ROUGH DRAFT

There should be a point to any writing experience. It doesn't help a child to say to him, *"Write anything at all. Just give me a page or two on anything you're thinking."* That would be hard for anyone to do. The first draft of any paper should be the child's thoughts about the assignment. He is thinking about what the exercise is going to teach him and how to complete it and learn the skills presented. We shouldn't look at that first draft and comment about anything other than his thinking about the subject. Don't worry about spelling or periods or upper case letters or commas. That comes just before the final draft.

Now is the time to compliment your child on his thinking. *"I can see you have thought about this subject some. Did this occur to you? How about this? I like your thinking here, nice touch. What a wonderful idea you had at this point. I sure would like to see more about that."*

After reading the first draft, you should give your child directions for further explorations of his ideas. General comments about the flavor of his work, or encouragement to re-examine his thinking, or new avenues of thought that might produce what you feel should be explored in the exercise.

As long as your child is trying to do as the directions indicate, your comments at this point should all be positive and very supportive. If you say, *"That sure is a mess, I don't know if I can read it at all. Where are the capital letters for the start of the sentences? Why is this all one paragraph?"* you will discourage your child and you may produce a reluctant writer.

SECOND ROUGH DRAFT

Your child has taken your encouragement and advice and rewritten his first draft. Now there should be some form to the writing. You should be able to tell whether your child is doing as the directions suggest. The directions in *Writing Strands* are very explicit, and you should expect your child to follow them, or you can change them and have your child follow yours. In either case, you should see in the second draft how your child is producing writing consistent with the objectives listed at the beginning of each exercise.

This draft is where you can look for the details that will produce a well written third rough draft or final draft. Now check for the ideas as they flow through the sentences. Look for paragraphing. Make suggestions about redundancies, and awkward phrases. Mention accidental rhyming and check for clichés. This is the kind of help your child needs at this point. If you see that the assignment is brief enough to not need more than three drafts, you might suggest that your child check the spelling and punctuation before the final copy is written.

FINAL COPY OR DRAFT

After your child has rewritten the second draft using your suggestions, you should ask to see it before it's turned in to you as completed. If your child wants to take the chance on using ink, that's no problem. You should be able to catch little problems and point them out in this last draft. If you feel it is important that you have a finished paper to keep on file, then you can ask that the paper be written in ink and made *perfect*.

Remember, these are children we're working with, and they can't be expected to do perfect work until they are our age. Keep a listing in your *Writing Strands* book of the problems that you and your child will solve in the future. They can't all be solved this week. It will be hard, but it's important that you have patience with misuse of apostrophes until you get to them. One problem solved each week will, in two years, produce almost error-free writing.

FORMATTING

In most university classes, the instructors will tell the students what style sheet to use for the papers done for each class. If this isn't done, the university library will have style sheets recommended by the various departments.

We don't teach term paper writing in the *Writing Strands* books because there's very little demand for that in college. Some of the very traditional schools may still ask for term papers, but most do not. They ask for papers. These are the explanatory and argumentative papers in levels six and seven. About 95% of the writing in college will be in these two modes. Your child will have to do research and incorporate that in the papers, but not with footnotes.

Your child's full name should be in the upper right corner of the paper. Under that should be the assignment title or number. Under that should be the date.

There should be a title with the major words capitalized on the first line of the paper. The title should **never** be underlined unless the words are also the title of a book. Then there should be one skipped line before the body of the paper.

The top, side, and bottom margins should all be the same size. This is usually one inch. Paper is cheap. Final drafts of papers written after the eighth grade should be double spaced and typed if possible. Only white paper should be used and only one side should be written on.

The pages after the first page should be numbered in the center at the bottom of the page. There should **never** be the words *The End* written at the end of any paper or story.

SPELLING RULES

In the *Writing Strands* books there are pages for you to keep track of your children's spelling problems. We recommend that you make each of your children an expert at the spelling of only one word a week. If this word is pulled from their writing (a word they had chosen to use) then they will see that word as important to them and necessary to their writing. They'll perceive the need to know the spelling of that word.

If you look up the words with your children and show them the derivation of the words, (where they come from; Greek or Latin, whether its background is German or French or English) and the prefixes and suffixes that apply and the connotations of the words (how we feel about them), your children can become experts in those words this week. If you have each child make cards with the word boldly printed on them and they are put up on the end of their beds, on their mirrors, in the bathroom, at their places for dinner and where they do their homeschooling, they will become immersed in those words and never lose their correct spelling.

Next week pick another word from each of their writings that they feel they need to know and don't know the spelling of and have them become experts in those words. In this way, in a few years, your children will have good vocabularies of words that they use that they can spell and you have eliminated all of the anxiety and failure with memorizing and testing of spelling lists. All of the research shows that learning spelling words in abstracted listings stays with a child only until the test and then is lost. Only short term memory is used in such exercises. The average adult in this country has a spelling vocabulary of about 300 words. Don't expect young children to have too much more than that.

The above exercises and the following listing of spelling rules should make good practical spellers of your children.

These rules have exceptions but they are not difficult to learn and are easily mastered. Once your children have learned these few rules, they should keep them from making the most common spelling errors; in addition, the rules will assist them in determining the spelling of unfamiliar words.

ie and *ei*:

Write *ie* when the sound is long *e*, except after *c*.

Examples: believe, field, niece, ceiling, receive, conceit

Exceptions: size, either, neither, weird

Write *ei* when the sound is not long *e*, especially when the sound is long *a*.

83

Examples: freight, weight, reign, forfeit, height

Exceptions: friend, mischief, conscience

Only one word ends in -*sede* - *supersede*; all other words of similar sound end in -*cede*.

Examples: precede, recede, secede, accede, concede

Adding Prefixes

A prefix is one or more letters or syllables added to the beginning of a word to change its meaning.

When a prefix is added to a word, the spelling of the word itself remains the same.

Examples: dis + satisfy = dissatisfy
mis + spell = misspell
in + numerable = innumerable
re + commend = recommend

Adding Suffixes

A suffix is one or more letters or syllables added to the end of a word to change its meaning.

When the suffixes -*ness* and -*ly* are added to a word, the spelling of the word itself is not changed.

Examples: plain + ness = plain*ness*
casual + ly = casua*lly*

Exceptions: Words ending in *y* usually change the *y* to *i* before -*ness* and -*ly*; empty - empt*iness*; heavy -heav*iness*; busy -bus*ily*; ordinary -ordinar*ily*. One-syllable adjectives ending in y generally do not change in spelling: dry - *dryness*; shy - *shyly*.

Drop the final e **before a suffix beginning with a consonant.**

Examples: truly, argument, acknowledgment, judgment

Exceptions: love + ly = lov*ely* hope + ful = hop*eful*
place + ment = plac*ement* care + less = car*eless*

With words ending in *y* preceded by a consonant change the *y* to *i* before any suffix not beginning with *i*.

Examples: accompany + ment = accompan*i*ment
plenty + ful = plent*i*ful
satisfy + es = satisf*i*es

but

intensify + ing = intensifying
modify + ing = modifying

Double the final consonant before a suffix that begins with a vowel if both of the following conditions exist: 1) the word has only one syllable or is accented on the last syllable; 2) the word ends in a single consonant preceded by a single vowel.

Examples: swim + ing = swi*mm*ing (one-syllable word)
confer + ed = confe*rr*ed (accent on last syllable; single consonant and single vowel)
benefit + ed = benefited (accent not on last syllable)
confer + ence = con'ference (accent shifted; consonant not doubled)

Spelling of the plural of nouns.

1. The regular way to form the plural of a noun is to add an *s*.

Examples: dog, dogs   cat, cats   house, houses

2. The plural of some nouns is formed by adding *es*.

Add *es* to form the plural of nouns ending in *s, sh, ch, z,* and *x*. The *e* is necessary to make the plural forms pronounceable.

Examples: dress, dresses   box, boxes
sandwich, sandwiches   dish, dishes
waltz, waltzes   bus, buses

3. The plural of nouns ending in *y* *preceded by a consonant* is formed by changing the *y* to *i* and adding *es*.

Examples: country, countries   fly, flies
forgery, forgeries   theory, theories
comedy, comedies   salary, salaries

85

4. The plural of nouns ending in *y preceded by a vowel* is formed by adding an *s*.

Examples: boy, boys   journey, journeys
monkey, monkeys   toy, toys
tray, trays   buoy, buoys

5. The plural of most nouns ending in *f* or *fe* is formed by adding *s*. The plural of some nouns ending in *f* or *fe* is formed by changing the *f* to *v* and adding *s* or *es*.

Examples: Add *s:*   gulf, gulfs   safe, safes
roof, roofs   kerchief, kerchiefs

Change *f* to *v* and add *s* or *es:*
leaf, leaves   wife, wives
shelf, shelves   knife, knives

6. The plural of some nouns ending in *o preceded by a vowel* is formed by adding *s*; the plural of most nouns ending in *o preceded by a consonant* is formed by adding *es*.

Examples: *o* following a vowel:
studio, studios   radio, radios

o following a consonant:
potato, potatoes   hero, heroes

Exceptions: soprano, sopranos   solo, solos
piano, pianos   concerto, concertos
potato, potatoes   silo, silos

7. The plural of a few nouns is formed in irregular ways.

Examples: child, child*ren*   tooth, t*eeth*   goose, g*eese*
woman, wom*en* mouse, m*ice* ox, ox*en*

8. The plural of compound nouns written as one word is formed by adding *s* or *es*.

Examples: spoonful, spoonfuls   cupful, cupfuls
leftover, leftovers   strongbox, strongboxes

9. The plural of compound nouns consisting of a noun plus a modifier is formed by making the modified word plural.

The modified word is the one that tells what the entire compound word does, not what it is. The plural of notary public is *notaries public* (they are *notaries*, not *publics)*; the plural of *mother-in-law* is *mothers-in-law* (they are *mothers*, not laws)

    Examples: runner-up, runners-up   editor in chief, editors in chief

10. The plural of a few compound nouns is formed in irregular ways.

    Examples: drive-in, drive-ins   six-year-old, six-year-olds
                  stand-by, stand-bys   tie-up, tie-ups

11. Some nouns are the same in the singular and the plural.

    Examples: sheep, deer, trout, salmon, Japanese, fowl

12. The plural of numbers, letters, signs, and words considered as words is formed by adding an apostrophe and an *s*.

    Examples: two *s*'s   two *4*'s   *and*'s   *that*'s
                  +'s   T's   *so*'s   1990's

THE FOLLOWING WORDS ARE OFTEN CONFUSED

already   *previously*
             I have *already* done my math.

all ready   all prepared
             Are you *all ready* for the math test?

altar   *a table or stand at which religious rites are performed*
             This is the *altar* used in the Communion service.

alter   *to change*
             Do not *alter* your plans because of that.

altogether *entirely*
             Mother is *altogether* against moving.

all together *all things in one place*
             The cups and plates will be *all together*.

brake   *a way to stop or slow down*
             The *brake* on your bike will stop you.

break   *to come apart*
Use this pencil but don't *break* it.

capital   *money used to start a business; the seat of* government
Lansing is the *capital* of Michigan. We have $200,000 *capital* to start the new business.

capitol   *office building where the government workers work*
I work at the *capitol*.

coarse   *rough; crude*
The homespun shirt was *coarse* and rough.

course   *path of action or passage or direction*
I like the *course* of action you have chosen.

complement *something that completes or makes whole*
fast forward is necessary to *complement* the team.

compliment *praise*
Janet's work deserves a *compliment*.

des'ert   *a dry area*
When the *desert* is irrigated things can grow.

desert'   *to leave*
Good soldiers don't *desert* their comrades.

dessert'   *last thing eaten at a good meal.*
My favorite *dessert* is ice cream.

its   *possessive form of it*
Our family must sell *its* second car.

it's   contraction of *it is*
It's time for dinner.

lead   (present tense) *going first*   The *lead* in the pencil is broken
We want you to *lead*   A metal used in pencils

led   (past tense) of *lead*
Bob *led* the way.

loose   free; not tight
The jacket is a *loose* fit.

lose   pronounced (looz) *to misplace*
Do not *lose* this money.

miner   *a mine worker*
The *miner* went into the hole.

minor   *under age; of little importance*
Minors cannot vote.
It is of *minor* importance.

personal   *individual; private*
My *personal* view is that we should go.

personnel   *group of people in the same company.*
Our company *personnel* would like that insurance plan.

plain   *not fancy; flat land; clear*
Plain clothes sometimes are best.
The *plain* stretched before the wagons.
Does this make things *plain* to you?

plane   *flat surface; airplane; a tool*
The flat part of the table is the *plane*.
The pilot got into the *plane*.
Use the *plane* to smooth the wood.

principal   *head of a school*; *the most important of a group*
The *principal* will talk to the students.
The *principal* reason is that I want to go.

principle   *a reason for a rule or a basic truth*
This computer chip works on a new *principle*.

quiet   *still; silent*
The hospital zone is a *quiet* zone.

quite	*completely; very* He was *quite* done. He is *quite* a hero.
route	*road; way to go* The *route* was well marked.
rout	*to run away* The retreat turned into a *rout*.
than	*a comparison* John is bigger *than* Jim.
then	*at that time* We ate *then we* did the dishes.
there	*at that place* We will be *there* soon.
their	*showing ownership* It will be *their* pool.
they're	(contraction) *they are* *They're* the kids to get the job done.
to	direction; connection Let's go *to* the lake. It should be glued *to* that piece.
too	*more than enough; also* I have eaten *too* much. I want to go, *too*.
two	*one + one* There are *two* boys who will help.
waist	*mid part of the body* Put the tape around your *waist*.
waste	*useless spending; material no longer of value* Do not *waste* your money on that book. That left over material is all *waste*.

weather   *what it's like outside*
What's the *weather* going to be?

whether   *a choice or alternative*
I don't know *whether* to go or not.

who's   (contraction) *who is*
It's John who's going.

whose   (possessive form of *who*)
Whose book is this?

your   (possessive form of *you*)
Is this book *your* book?

you're   (contraction of *you are*)
I hope *you're* feeling better.

Scope and Sequence

The series of books called *Writing Strands* and *Reading Strands* presents a complete language arts program in reading and composition. The exercises in *Writing Strands* are designed to teach four modes of writing: *argumentative, explanatory, creation* and *report*.

The assignments in the lower levels are not labeled as such, but they do teach the skills students will need to be able to write in these four modes. For instance, in Level Three, the second assignment, "Controlling Sentences and Paragraphs," is labeled *basic*. This means that this exercise teaches a skill that students will need in all four of the major modes. In the same way, the 11th assignment in Level Five teaches students to use detail in description. This is a skill that will be needed in later work. The exercises in levels 1-5 teach fundamental skills, and this listing indicates how the assignments feed into the four major modes.

Writing Strands Level 1

The package of the *Level 1* book and the tape for parents is designed to help children between the ages of 3 and 8 to learn that oral language is fun to use. And that's all it does—teach the fun of word use. Through games, projects, and programs, it encourages children to expect that the fun in oral word use will carry over to written work—an essential ingredient for writing skill.

Writing Strands Level 2

1. Adjectives
2. Listing
3. Reporting
4. Paragraphing
5. Ordering Actions
6. Grouping and Variety
7. Story Writing
8. Convincing
9. Writing Dialogue
10. Letter Writing
11. Personal Narration
12. Comparing
13. Greeting Cards
14. Projection
15. Imagination

Writing Strands Level 3

1. Following Directions (basic)
2. Sentence & Paragraph Control (basic)
3. Rewriting Sentences (basic)
4. Description (people)
5. Description (people's thoughts)
6. Organization (activities)
7. Organization (objects)
8. Description (perspective)
9. Story Creation (creation)
10. Description (organization)
11. Description (actions)
12. Narrative Events (organization)
13. Creation (narrative)

Writing Strands Level 4

1. How a Sentence Does It (basic)
2. Organization (idea connections)
3. Organization (main points)
4. Creation (emotions)
5. Organization (actions)
6. Narrative Voice (basic)
7. Changing Tenses (basic)
8. Paragraph Control (basic)
9. Description 1 (buildings)
10. Description 2 (buildings)
11. Description 3 (buildings)
12. Organization (thoughts)
13. Point of View (basic)
14. Tense Control (basic)
15. Changes (description)
16. Narrative Voice Location (basic)
17. Attitude in Description (NV)
18. Long and Short of It. (style)

Writing Strands Level 5

1. Narrative Attitude (basic)
2. Sentence Interest (creation)
3. Argument (organization)
4. Narrative Voice Knowledge (creation)
5. Active/Passive Voice (basic)
6. Narrative Voice Position (description)
7. Order (organization)
8. Dialogue (basic) (creation)
9. Reader Emotions (creation)
10. Tense Control (basic)
11. Details (description)
12. Flashback (organization)
13. Foreshadowing (organization)
14. Information Control (description)
15. Following A Scenario (organization)
16. Letters (organization)

Writing Strands Level 6

1. Character Traits (creation)
2. Organizing Ideas (report)
3. Creating Conflict (creation)
4. Point of View (explanatory essay)
5. Survey (report)
6. Book Report (report)
7. Personal Observation (report)
8. Interviewing (report)
9. Creating Characters (creation)
10. Decisions (creation)
11. Character Actions (creation)
12. Business Letters (organization)

Writing Strands Level 7

1. Moving Characters (creation)
2. Organizing Reports (report)
3. Describing For Purpose (creation)
4. Resolving Conflicts (creation)
5. Point of View (expository)
6. Controlling Readers (creation)
7. Reporting of Surveys (report, exposition)
8. Argumentative Exposition (essay)
9. Book Report (report)
10. Scientific Reports (report)
11. Interviewing (creation report)
12. Solving Problems (creation)
13. Emotional Reactions (creation)
14. Individualizing characters (creation)

Writing Exposition	Gives every type of assignment that students might be presented with in undergraduate college work. It also prepares students to write the essays for the essay portion of the SAT. It gives examples and directions for taking essay tests and writing the essays for placement in college freshman English classes. It has examples of the presented assignments written by very bright high school students. Presented are experiences in the following: writing manuals, examining literature, writing social studies reports, compare and contrast papers, reaction papers, biasing and propaganda recognition and production, term papers, decision making.

Communication and Interpersonal Relationships	
	Bridges the gap between the protected environment of homeschool and the adult world by giving student practice in personal communication skills.

Creating Fiction:	A very sophisticated approach to short fiction for high school and above. It is designed to prepare writers to send their work to publishers. It should be used only by those really interested in learning to write. It instructs in 17 aspects of creative writing and has very fine student work as examples of what the exercises might produce.

Reading Strands:	The non-writing half of language arts—reading and talking about the abstract ideas in the literature and interpreting the works for meaning. A manual for parents on how to discuss literature with young readers from five to eighteen years old. It has detailed directions in the Socratic methods of teaching and thousands of titles listed by age, grade, and reading level. Most of the book is composed of the techniques of interpretation with transcribed recordings of parents using the techniques with homeschooled children.

NOVELS

Dragonslaying Is For Dreamers with parents' manual for novel study.
Axel Meets The Blue Men
Axel's Challenge

These books are light fantasies about this young hero solving problems reaching maturity and making decisions based on value systems. This trilogy follows a boy as he fights dragons, saves his kingdom from invaders and teaches his son to value justice and honor.

Dragonslaying Is For Dreamers deals with the problems of a young man knowing when he has reached adulthood. (This book and the parenhts' teaching manual are also on audio tapes)
Axel Meets The Blue Men examines the problems of a person holding a value system when the rest of society exerts pressures for change.
Axel's Challenge demonstrates methods of making choices when values are in conflict.

INDEX

National Writing Institute Order Form

		Qty.	Total
❏	**Writing Strands Level 1** Oral work for ages 3-8 $14.95 ea.	___	___
❏	**Writing Strands Level 2** About 7 years old $18.95 ea.	___	___
❏	**Writing Strands Level 3** Starting program ages 8-12 $18.95 ea.	___	___
❏	**Writing Strands Level 4** Any age after Level 3 or starting program at age 13 or 14 $18.95 ea.	___	___
❏	**Writing Strands Level 5** Any age after Level 4 or starting program at age 15 or 16 $20.95 ea.	___	___
❏	**Writing Strands Level 6** 17 or any age after Level 5 $20.95 ea.	___	___
❏	**Writing Strands Level 7** 18 or any age after Level 6 $22.95 ea.	___	___
❏	**Writing Exposition** Senior high school and after Level 7 $22.95 ea.	___	___
❏	**Creating Fiction** Senior high school and after Level 7 $22.95 ea.	___	___
❏	**Evaluating Writing** Parents' manual for all levels of *Writing Strands* $19.95 ea.	___	___
❏	**Reading Strands** Parents' manual for story and book interpretation, all grades $22.95 ea.	___	___
❏	**Communication and Interpersonal Relationships** Communication manners (teens) $17.95 ea.	___	___
❏	**Dragonslaying Is for Dreamers - package** 1st novel in *Dragonslaying* trilogy (early teens) and parents' manual for analyzing the novel. $18.95 ea.	___	___
❏	**Dragonslaying Is for Dreamers - novel only** $9.95 ea.	___	___
❏	**Axel Meets the Blue Men** 2nd novel in *Dragonslaying* trilogy (teens) $9.95 ea.	___	___
❏	**Axel's Challenge** Final novel in *Dragonslaying* trilogy(teens) $9.95 ea.	___	___
❏	**Dragonslaying trilogy** All three novels in series $25.00 set	___	___

SUBTOTAL: ___

Texas residents add **7.75%** sales tax ___

U.S. Shipping: $2.00 per book (**$4.00 Minimum**) .... ___

Outside U.S. Shipping: $4.00 per book (**$8.00 Minimum**) .... ___

TOTAL U.S. FUNDS:

❏ CHECK or MONEY ORDER .... ___

❏ CREDIT CARD .... ___

❏ VISA   ❏ DIICOVER   ❏ MasterCard

Account Number

☐☐☐☐ - ☐☐☐☐ - ☐☐☐☐ - ☐☐☐☐

Expiration date: Month ☐☐   Year ☐☐

_____
Signature

(PLEASE PRINT) We ship U.P.S. to the 48 states, so please no P.O. #.

Name: _____

Street: _____

City: _____

State: _____ Zip: _____

Phone: (_____) _____

E-Mail (if available) _____

SHIPPING INFORMATION

Continental US : We ship via UPS ground service. Most customers will receive their orders within 10 business days.

Alaska, Hawaii, US Military addresses and US territories: We ship via US Priority Mail. Orders generally arrive within 2 weeks.

Canada: We ship via Air Mail. Most customers receive orders within 2 weeks.

Other international destinations: We generally ship via Air Mail. Delivery times vary.

RETURNS

Our books are guaranteed to please you. If they do not, return them within 30 days and we'll refund the full purchase price.

PRIVACY

We respect your privacy. We will not sell, rent or trade your personal information.

INQUIRIES AND ORDERS:

Phone:	(800) 688-5375 TOLLFREE
Fax:	(888) 663-7855 TOLLFREE
Write:	**National Writing Institute** 624 W. University #248 Denton, TX 76201-1889
E-mail:	info@writingstrands.com
Website:	www.writingstrands.com

NEW ADDRESS